Paper Boxes

First published in the United States of America by:
Quarry Books, an imprint of
Rockport Publishers, Inc.
146 Granite Street
Rockport, Massachusetts 01966-1299
Telephone: (508) 546-9590
Fax: (508) 546-7141

Distributed to the book trade and art trade in the United States by:
North Light, an imprint of
F & W Publications
1507 Dana Avenue
Cincinnati, Ohio 45207
Telephone: (513) 531-2222

ISBN 1-56496-277-6

10 9 8 7 6 5 4 3 2 1

Designer
Kristen Webster
Blue Sky Limited

Photography
Michael Lafferty

Manufactured in Hong Kong by Excel Printing

Paper Boxes

Michael G. LaFosse

QUARRY BOOKS
Rockport, Massachusetts

Contents

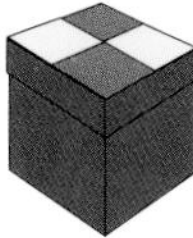
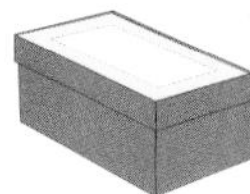
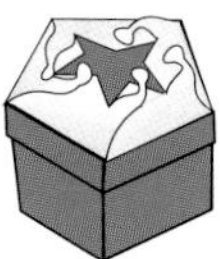

Introduction

The projects in this book were designed to be fun and simple to make. Easy to construct from almost any type of paper, these eight projects provide a versatile platform for creative invention. Triangle, square, rectangle, pentagon, hexagon, heart: all of these basic box shapes have been addressed in this volume. The box designs and presentation ideas range from the classic to the unusual and offer something to suit every occasion.

Our method will allow you to produce winning results from even the most ordinary papers. Experiment with the paper provided, then use the blank tracing patterns in the back of the book to create boxes from a wide variety of paper and other materials. The folded double-wall construction provides added support to the box walls, as well as a neat, finished rim. Each of the box lid patterns has a reinforced rim and our unique appliqué slot system, which allows for the insertion of an infinite variety of decorative paper elements to customize your own creations. An added bonus is that these boxes are super simple to make and a lot of fun, too! You will enjoy experimenting with the possibilities provided by different paper and after a time you may go beyond the scope of this book and apply these techniques to create dozens of other boxes and containers of your own, whether as gifts or for use around the home or office.

Enjoy!
—Michael G. LaFosse

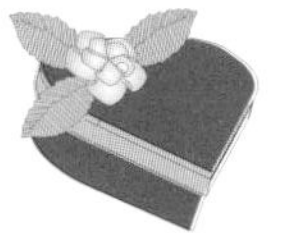  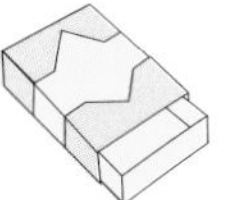 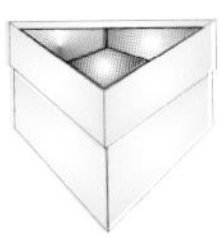

How to Use This Book

Each box project begins with a list of materials and a picture of the finished box. The papers provided are marked with folding lines for your first attempts, and the templates in the back of the book can be traced to make an endless supply of box patterns. To get the best possible results, the three most important things to keep in mind are: cut slowly and carefully, fold precisely, and get to know the key. The key on page 9 explains the fold lines and arrows (known as the Yoshizawa/Randlet standardized origami system) that accompany each drawing in this book. If you are already familiar with this system of folding notation you will feel right at home; otherwise, spend a few moments learning to recognize these symbols and to understand the terminology.

Begin by cutting out all paper elements for the desired project from the supply sheets provided at the back of the book. You may want to photocopy both the pattern sheets and the templates, so that you will have extras for practice or in case of a mistake. Protect your work surface by placing a piece of cardboard under anything you are cutting with a blade. For most projects in this book you will find that using a tool (such as a letter opener) and a straightedge (such as a ruler) to score the fold lines on the box elements will make folding much easier and more accurate.

Study the step-by-step photos carefully, to visually check your work. It is often helpful to look ahead at the next diagram or photo to see the results of a fold in advance. Take time to perform the folds neatly and accurately.

Though adhesives are not always necessary, you may wish to make your creations last longer by adding a little white glue or paste at key contact points. Apply adhesives sparingly and neatly, and have a damp cloth handy to wipe away any spills.

Blue tracing patterns are included for each project, so that you can make additional boxes from whatever materials you choose. The showcase at the end of each project offers variations on each box, for added inspiration.

How to Make Box Lids

Making the lid is the trickiest part of making a paper box. Although each of the ten featured boxes has a different shape, the six step technique outlined below can be applied to any of the box lids in the book. Once you have mastered the basic rules for constructing a lid, you will easily be able to follow the more detailed instructions that accompany each project. Have fun!

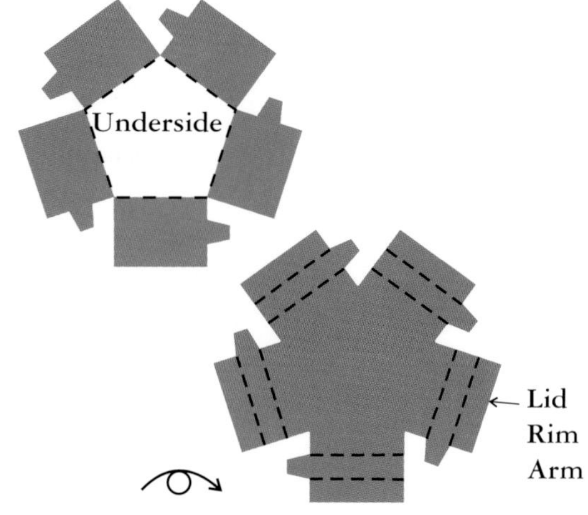

1 Valley-fold on the dashed lines of the underside of the lid paper cutout. Turn the paper over.

2 Valley-fold along the dashed lines. Each rectangular extension is referred to as a lid-rim arm.

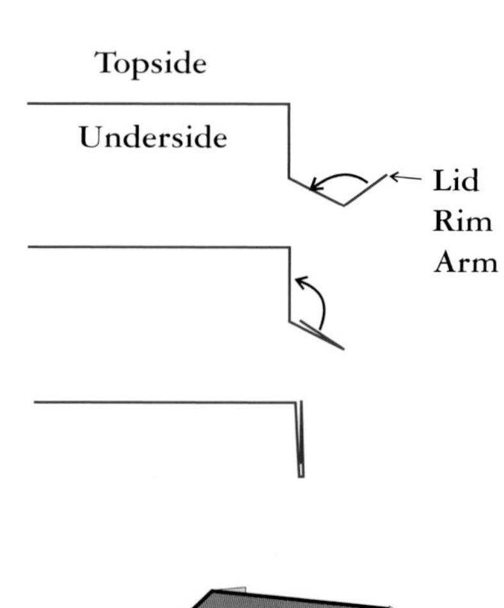

3 (Side view of one lid-rim arm) Valley-fold the outermost segment of the lid-rim arm against the middle segment.

4 Valley-fold this double layer of paper against the innermost segment of the lid-rim arm. Set this three-layer lid rim at right angles to the top of the lid.

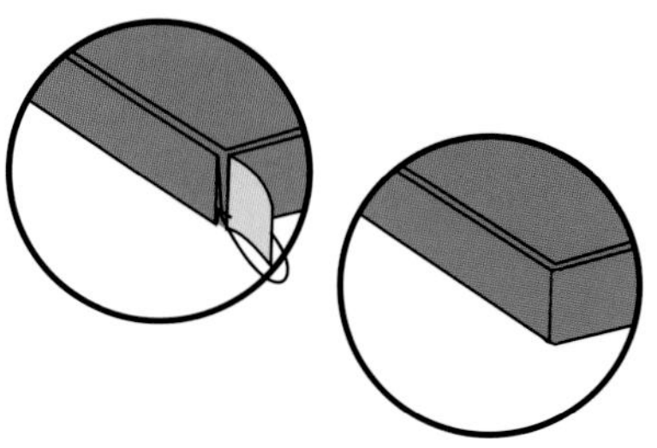

5 Apply paste to the outside of the exposed tabs. Tuck each pasted tab into its adjacent open lid-wall edge. Press firmly to seal. Allow the lid to dry on the box base.

Glossary & Key

Because the illustrations can show only a segment of a project's folding procedure, it is helpful to know whether the paper is being folded in front or from behind. The origami system of Valley-folds and Mountain-folds uses two kinds of broken lines (see key diagram) to show when to fold toward the project's surface (valley-fold) and when to fold behind the surface (mountain-fold).

Valley-fold—Relative to the displayed view of the paper being folded, a valley-fold is always folded in front of the project's surface. If you were to unfold a valley-fold you would see a valley-crease, which dents into the paper's surface, forming a valley.

Mountain-fold—Relative to the displayed view of the paper being folded, a mountain-fold is always folded behind the project's surface. If you were to unfold a mountain-fold you would see a mountain-crease, which rises up from the paper's surface, forming a mountain ridge.

Various types of arrows help make the folding instructions even clearer. These arrows are easy to understand with a quick study of the illustrated key. Whenever you see the repeat arrow in a diagram, you must apply the demonstrated folding procedure to all indicated parts of the project.

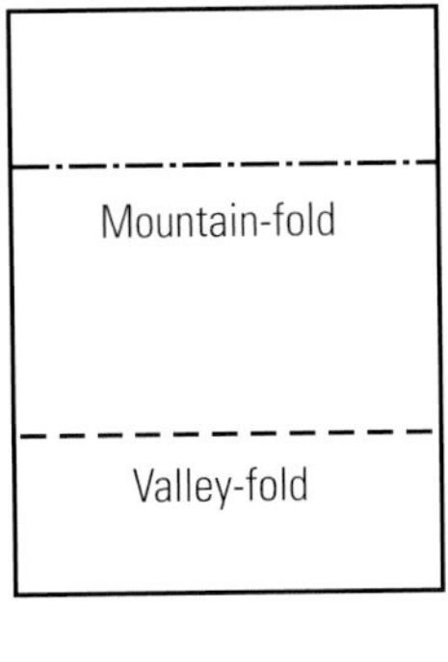

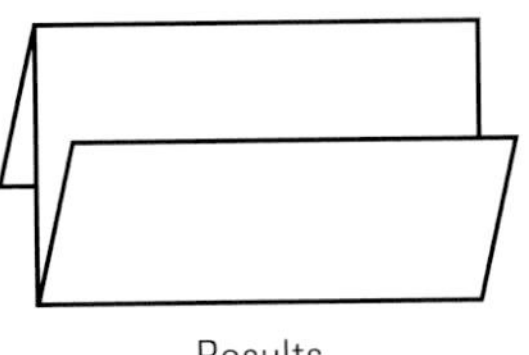

Results

Standard Symbols

—·—·—·—·—·—·—·—

Mountain-fold

– – – – – – – – – – – –

Valley-fold

Directional Arrows

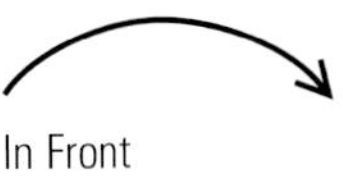

In Front

Behind

Turn Model Over

Insert/Apply Pressure

Repeat

Enlarged View

Triangle Box

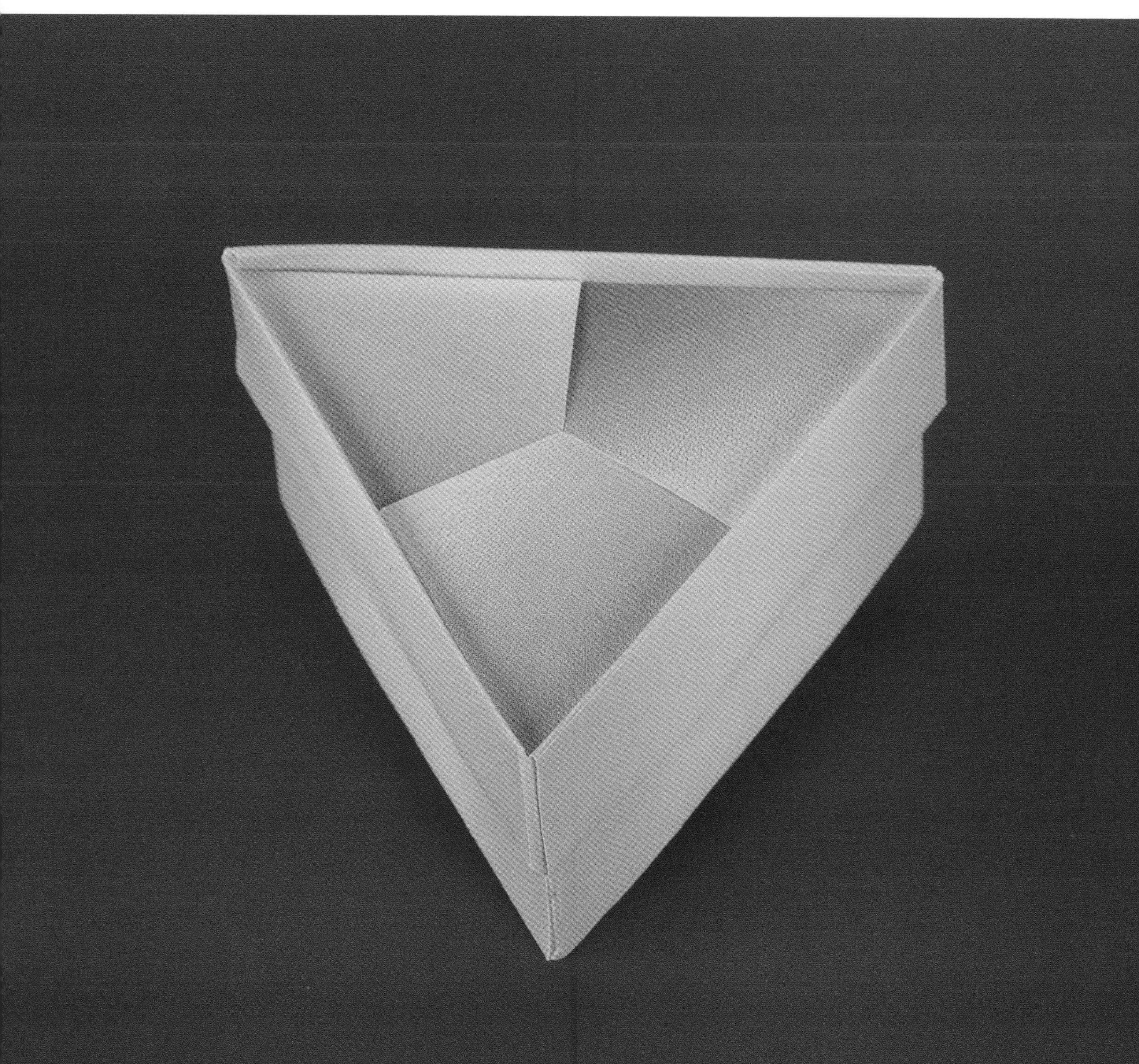

How to Build a Triangle Box

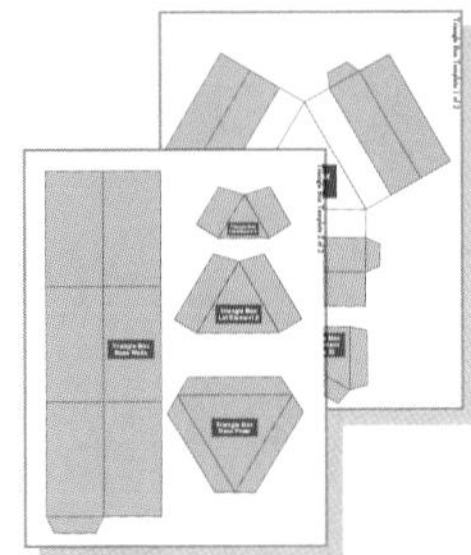

This unusual box has two interesting features: First, the top perimeter of the lid is slightly raised above the lid surface. This is possible because you can vary the dimensions of the rectangular perimeter fold segments. Second, when designing decorative paper inserts for any lid, you may choose to develop shapes from the edges or from the corners of the lid's shape. An example of each is provided with this project.

The triangle shape is not the most economical form for a box to contain most gift objects. However, you will find that nothing presents a very small and special item so well as the equilateral triangle. Choose a gift that is at least one-third the size of the inside dimensions of the box and add some beautiful cushion material. The special gift will shine!

Materials

- *Triangle Box paper elements*
- *Scissors and/or X-Acto knife*
- *Paste or glue stick*
- *Brush for applying paste*

Triangle Box Tips

- *Use sharp scissors or a pointed razor knife with a fresh blade to cut out the paper pieces. This will give you cleaner edges and a better-looking box.*
- *When removing paper pieces, cut from the back side of the paper provided. Cut just inside the outlines and fold exactly on the indicated crease lines.*
- *It will not be necessary to glue the ornamental lid elements to the top of the lid. This will enable you to switch the patterns whenever you wish.*
- *If you make more boxes from heavyweight paper, be sure to pre-crease all fold lines by scoring with a straightedge and blade. Be prepared to make trimming adjustments to account for the extra thickness of the material.*
- *Use white paste instead of liquid glue for this project. Use only the smallest amount to prevent warping.*

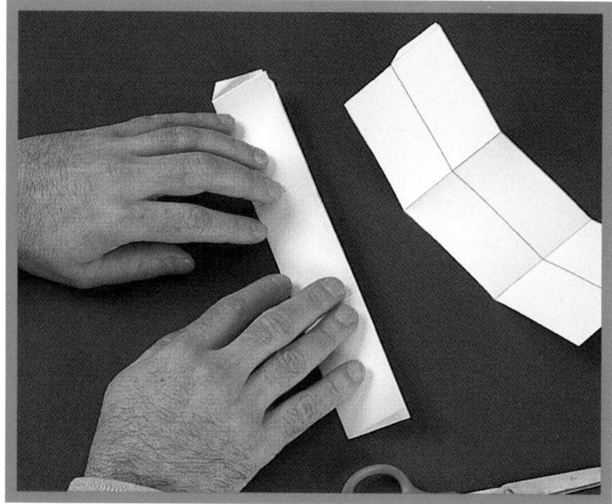

1 Valley-fold the short lines of the base wall; then carefully align the opposing long edges and fold in half so that the colored side of the paper shows. Repeat with the other base wall element. Make the folded edges sharp and clean by running the side of your thumbnail along the folded paper.

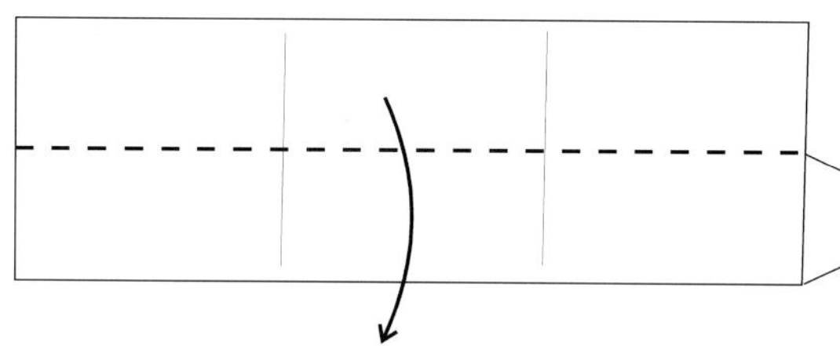

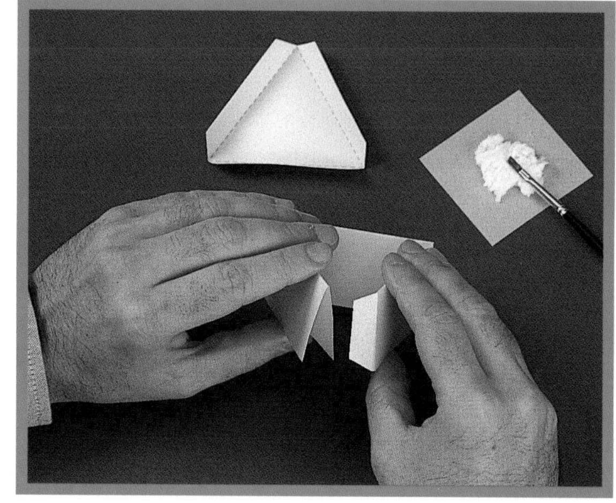

2 Apply paste to the outside of the exposed tab and bring the two short ends of the base wall element together.

3 Tuck the pasted tab in between the folded layers of the end of the paper and press firmly to make a good fit. This forms the walls of the base of the box. The top of this triangular form has a folded edge and the bottom has an open, double edge of paper.

Make the floor of the box by folding the tabs to stand vertically around the triangular edge of the base bottom. Apply paste to both sides of each tab, then attach the floor to the wall by carefully fitting the tabs of the floor into the open edges of the base wall element.

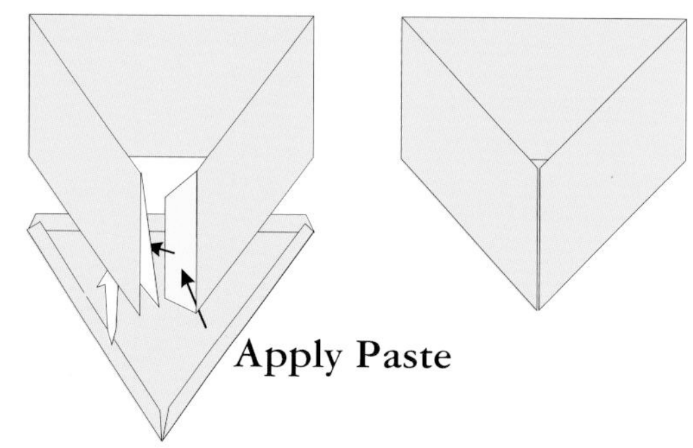

4 Carefully fold the edges of the lid. Begin with the underside (the side of the lid paper with the white triangle) and valley-fold the innermost creases. Unfold and turn the paper over. Make the valley-folds indicated and crease them to close at right angles to the top of the lid.

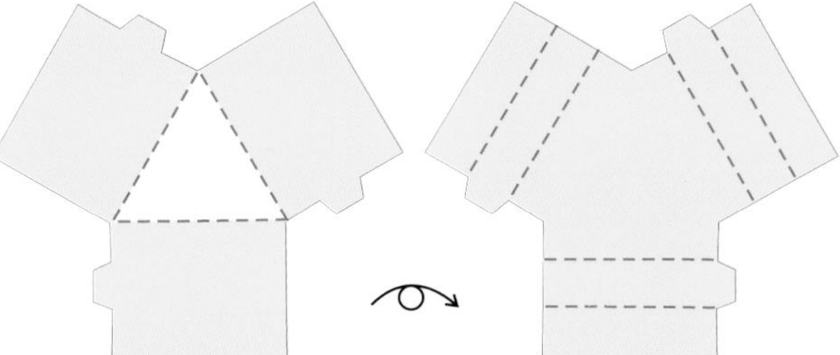

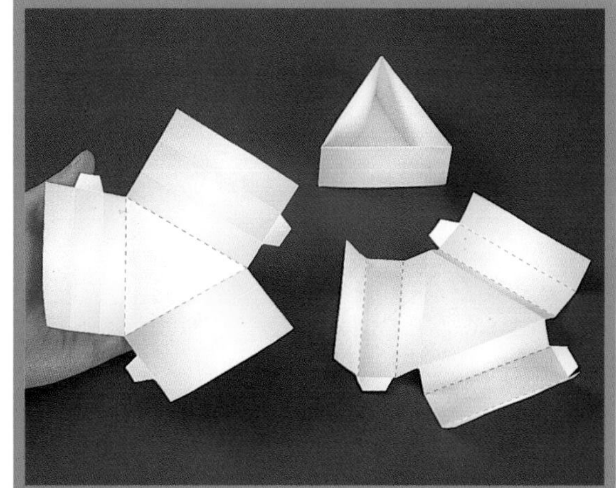

5 Apply paste to one or both sides of each tab. Tuck each pasted tab into its adjacent open lid-wall edge. Press firmly to seal. Allow the lid to dry on the box base.

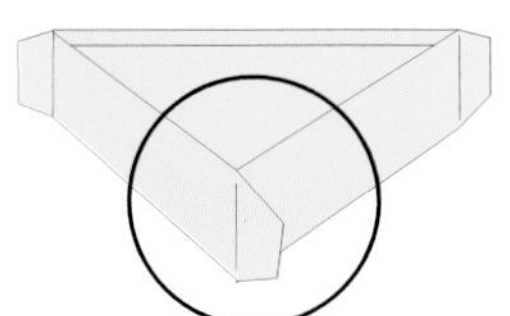

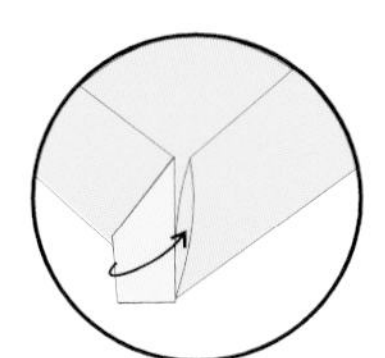

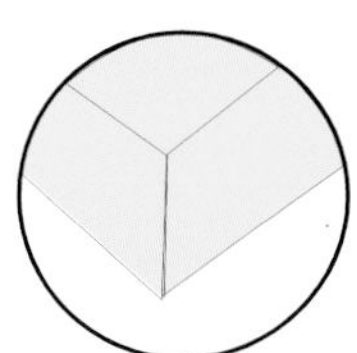

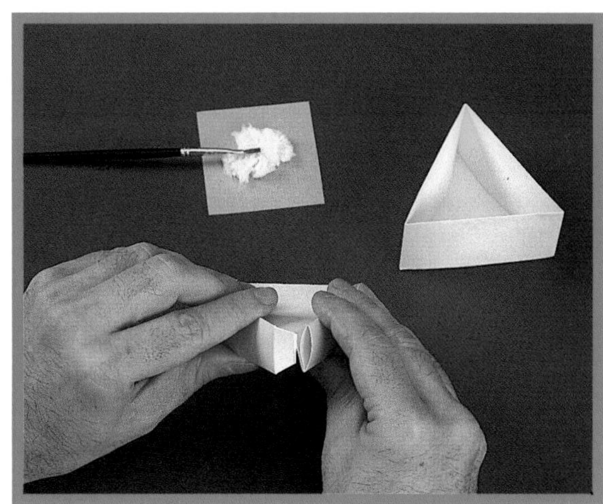

6 There are two possible lid patterns included here. The equilateral triangle inserts make a striped pattern, the three right-angle inserts make a three-cornered pattern. Begin by folding the tabs on the indicated crease lines of all color inserts. Square the folded tabs so that they are at right angles to the face edge of the paper form.

For the equilateral triangle set of inserts, lay the small shape over the larger shape. Tuck the tabs into the open edges in the perimeter of the box lid so that the result is a three-colored stripe pattern across the top of the box.

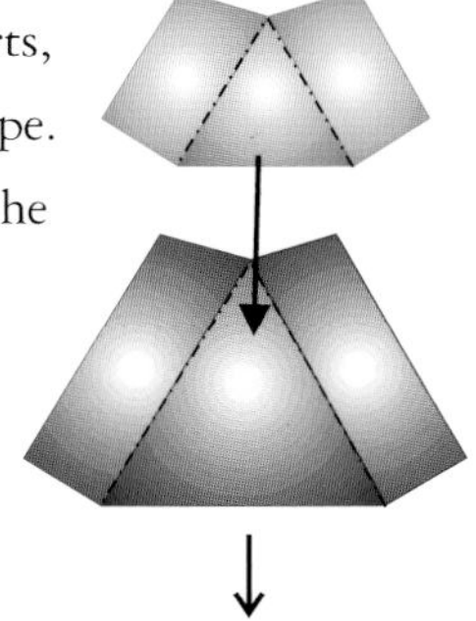

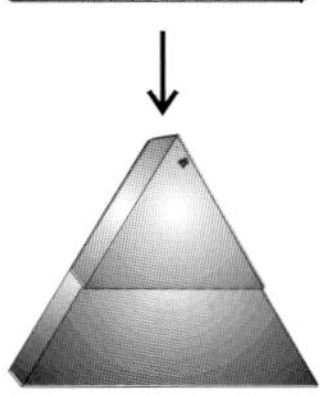

7 For the three-colored, right-angle set of inserts, arrange the pieces in a centered, overlapping manner by tucking the pointed end of each triangle under the wide end of the next one. Square the folded tabs so that they are at right angles to the face edge of the paper form. You should end up with the three colors evident in identical four-sided shapes.

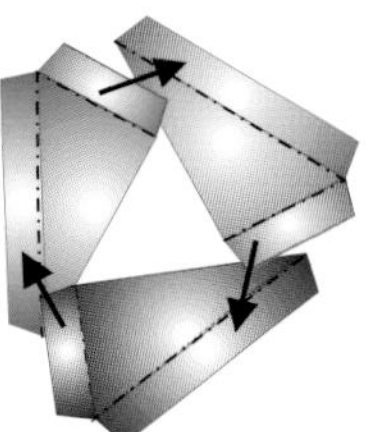

8 Tuck the tabs into the open edges in the perimeter of the box lid. This is an example of pattern development from the edges of the lid shape (see photo showcase for other treatments).

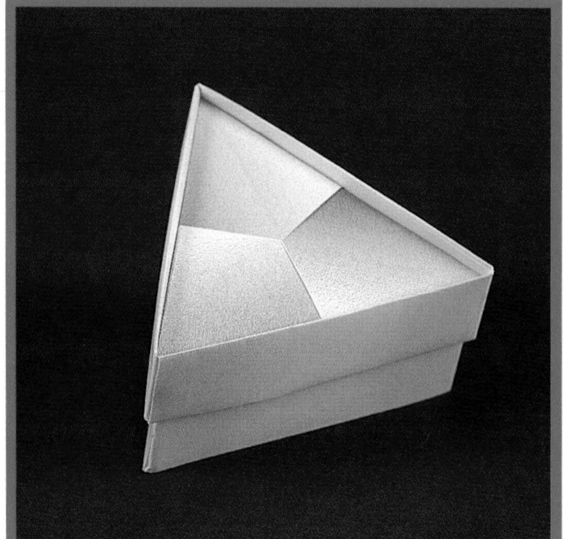

9 The finished triangle box. How many other ornamental lid insert designs can you come up with?

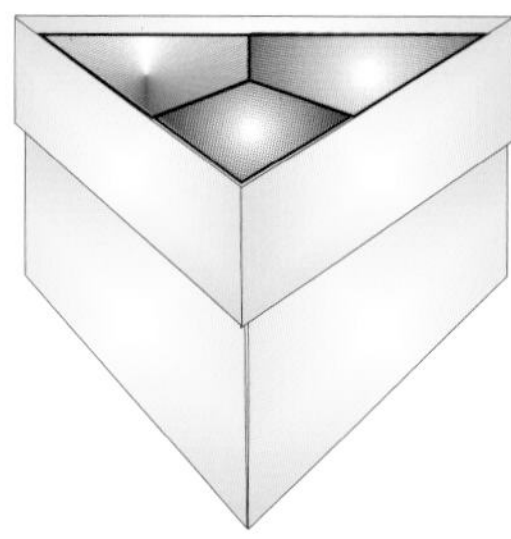

Triangle Box Gallery

You can scale this canister set to any size, for an attractive storage system. Use heavy paper to make large sets.

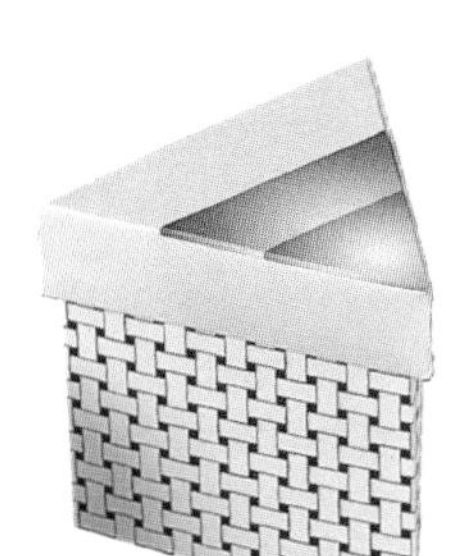

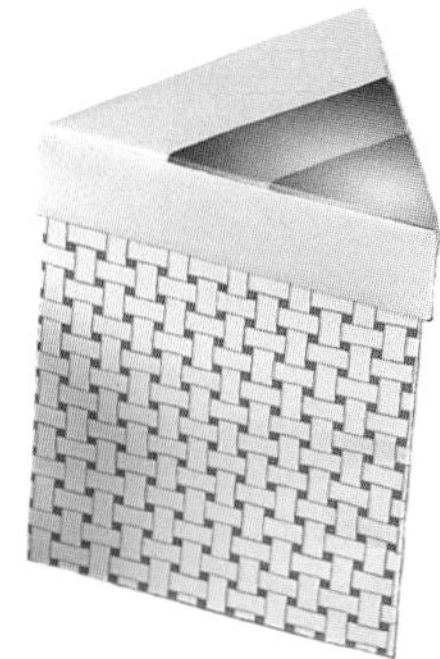

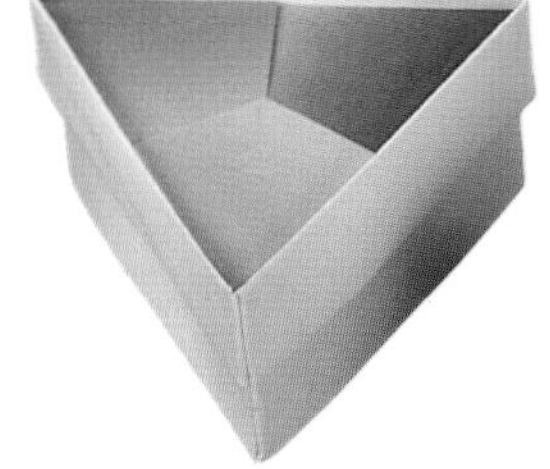

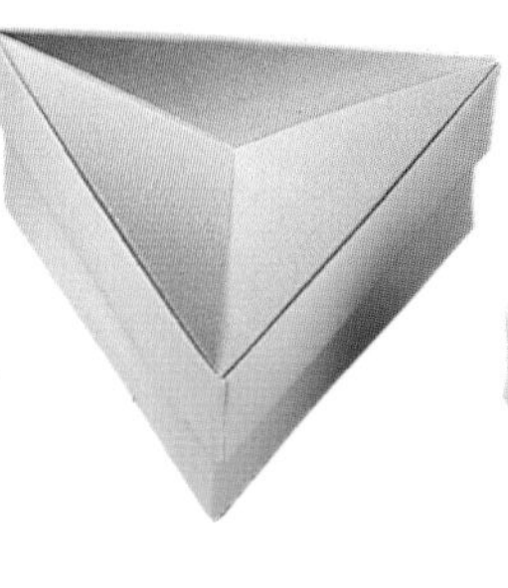

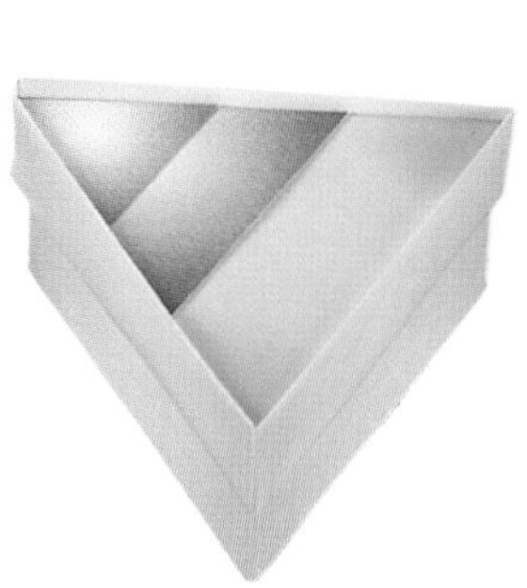

Tri-colored lids from modular elements. There are many possible arrangements for these elements. Feel free to experiment with them. This model is stackable and would make an attractive small organizer set.

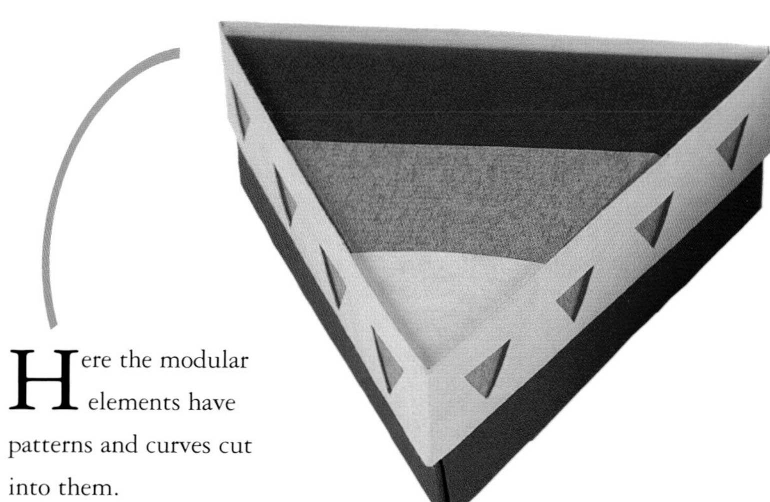

Here the modular elements have patterns and curves cut into them.

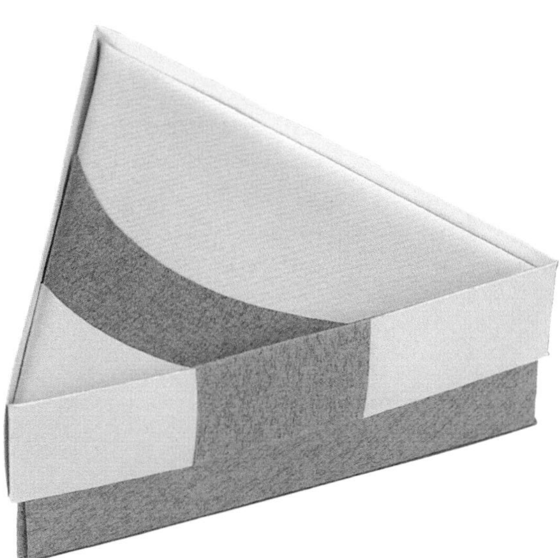

Cube Box

How to Build a Cube Box

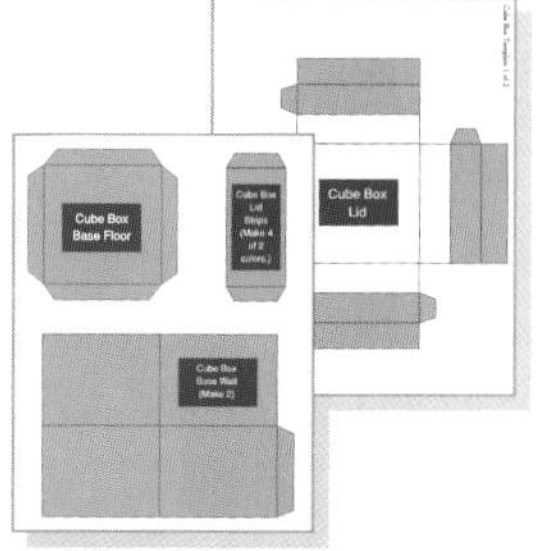

These perfectly square containers combine utility with simplicity and beauty. Make several cube boxes to "nest" or stack together, or use paper in primary colors to make a set with different color tops and bottoms. If you prefer patterned to plain papers, use simple, bold designs to highlight the perfect geometry of the cube. Pair textured and glossy papers for a subtle contrast between boxes and lids of the same color. You can also weave two solid colors together to give the lid a checkerboard or triangle pattern.

Cube Box Tips

- *Use a straightedge and a razor knife to cut neat edges for the decorative lid elements.*
- *It is not necessary to glue the ornamental lid elements into the top of the lid. This will enable you to switch the patterns whenever you wish.*
- *Allow extra distance between the inside of the fold lines of the decorative lid elements if you make boxes from heavier paper.*
- *To make a nesting set, photocopy the pattern on a copier with a zoom function. Reduce or enlarge by 15% for a perfect fit.*

Materials

- *Cube Box paper elements*
- *Scissors and/or X-Acto knife*
- *Paste or glue stick*
- *Brush for applying paste*

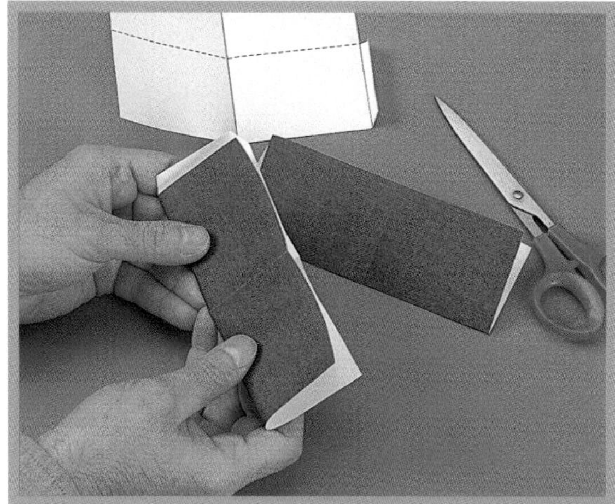

1 Valley-fold the short lines of the base wall; then carefully align the opposing long edges and fold in half so that the colored side of the paper shows. Repeat with the other base wall element. Make the folded edges sharp and clean by running the side of your thumbnail along the folded paper.

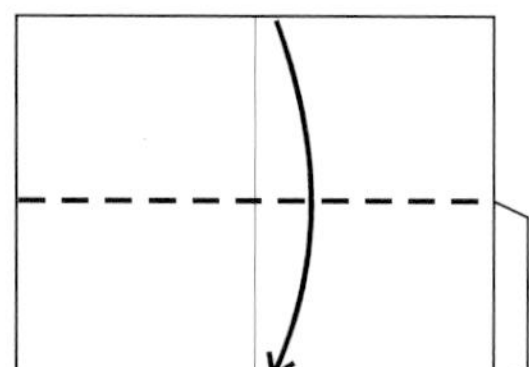

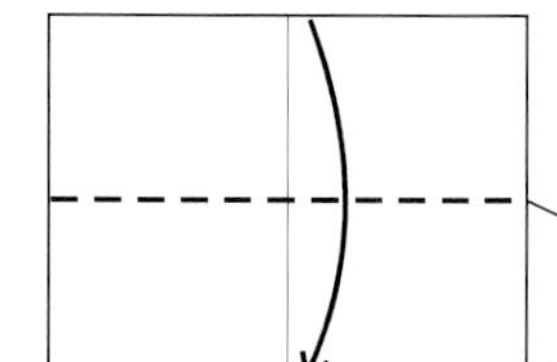

2 Apply paste to the outside of one of the tabs. The outside of a tab is on the same side as the colored side of the paper. Connect the two base wall elements together, end to end, by inserting the pasted tab of one between the folded layers of the other. The pasted tab should stick to only one inside surface of the base wall element.

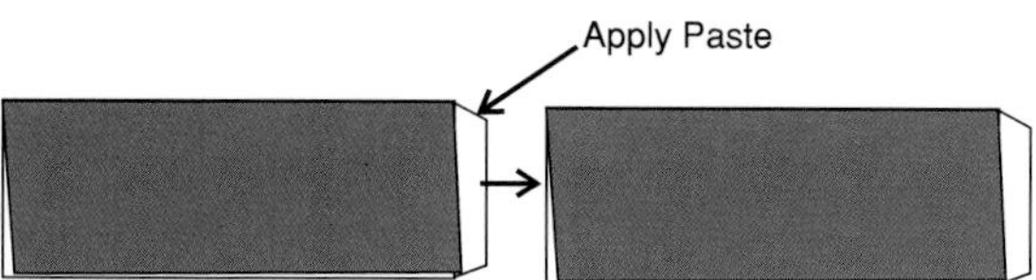

3 Apply paste to the outside of the exposed tab and bring the two ends of the base wall element together. Tuck the pasted tab between the folded layers of the end of the paper and press firmly to make a good fit.

4 Make the cube even by adjusting the creases. This is the base wall of the box: The top edge is folded; the bottom is an open, double edge of paper. The tabs of the floor will be pasted between the open edges of paper.

Fold the tabs of the box floor, as shown, apply paste, and carefully insert into the base wall.

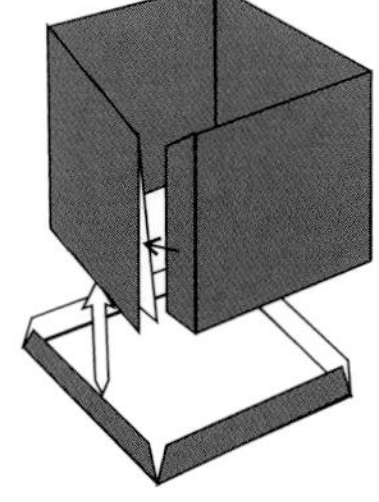

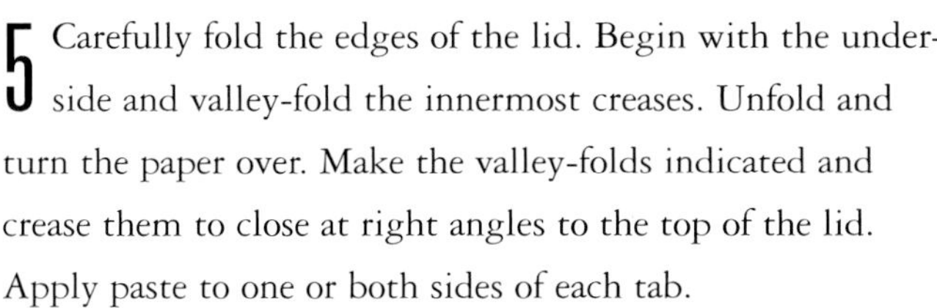

5 Carefully fold the edges of the lid. Begin with the underside and valley-fold the innermost creases. Unfold and turn the paper over. Make the valley-folds indicated and crease them to close at right angles to the top of the lid. Apply paste to one or both sides of each tab.

6 Tuck each pasted tab into its adjacent open lid-wall edge. Press firmly to seal. Allow the lid to dry on the box base.

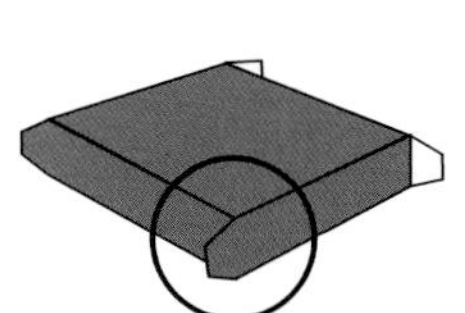
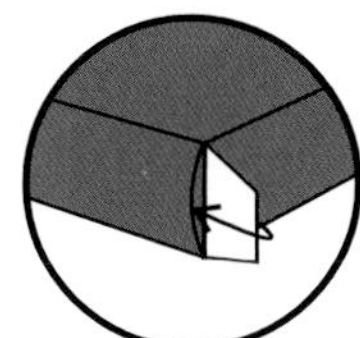
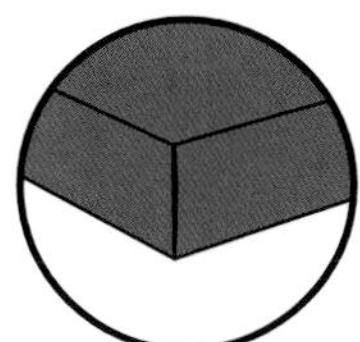

7 Fold the tab edge on each of the lid elements. Make this fold very sharp and clean. Weave the four elements, alternating the colors, and fold tab edges at right-angles to the finished checkerboard top.

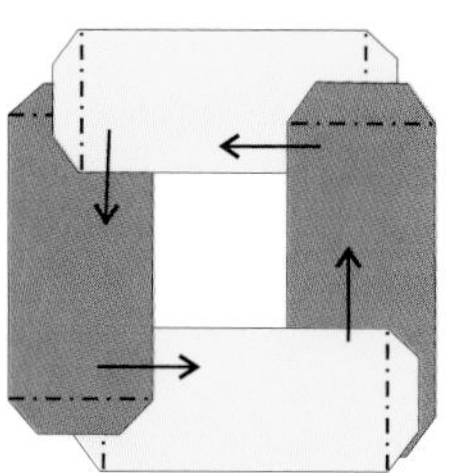

8 Insert tab edge (with or without paste at first) into the open edges of the perimeter of the box lid.

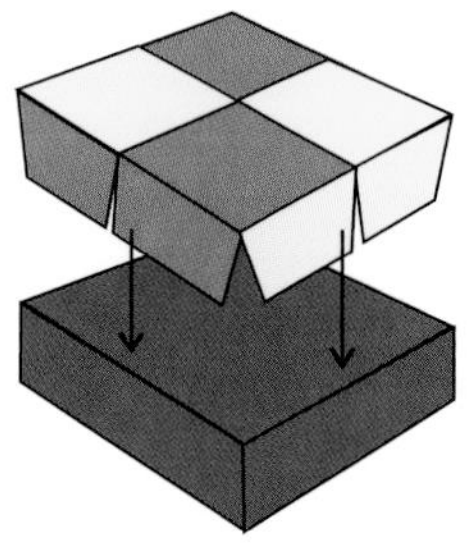

9 The finished puzzle box. You may further divide the colored strips and re-weave for smaller and more numerous checks.

Cube Box Gallery

Each of these colorful nesting boxes is fifteen percent smaller than the size before it. Use the zoom function of a photocopy machine to reduce or enlarge the pattern for different sizes.

These checkerboards are created by cutting narrower strips and basket-weaving the top of the lid. Be sure to make strips that are even and clean-cut.

Simple, bold patterns are very effective for this project. The woven triangle pattern was created by cutting out four triangle-shaped elements, with tabs. Each triangle is the size of one-quarter of the lid, when a line is drawn diagonally from one corner to an opposite corner.

Frame Box

How to Build a Frame Box

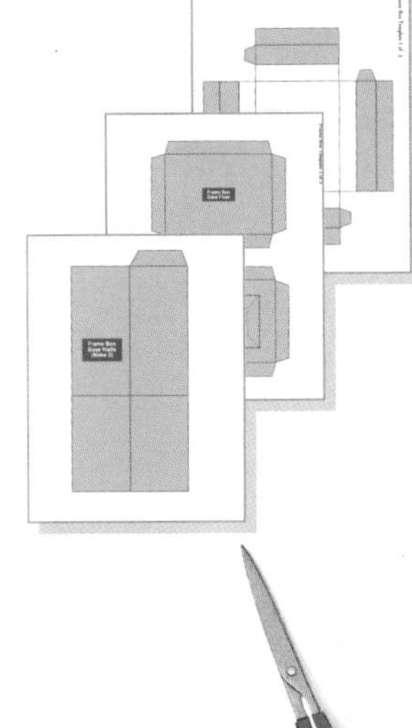

This box is the perfect container for treasures, keepsakes, or souvenirs. A cut-out in the lid lets you frame photographs, or scrapbook items such as invitations, theater tickets, newspaper clippings, wedding or birth announcements, or any other mementos you hold dear. Frame a baby picture and keep a lock of hair or first tooth in the box. Send a gardener friend a box of seeds with the seed packet framed on the lid. The frame box is wonderfully adaptable for all sorts of little gifts and special occasions.

Frame Box Tips

- *This is a good box to make from heavier materials such as textured, cover-weight papers. Use a ruler and letter opener or similar tools to pre-score such materials to make folding easier.*
- *If you pre-score the folding edges of the inside of the frame opening, you will get neater and more accurate results.*
- *Allow a little more distance between the inside of the fold lines of the frame if you make boxes from heavier paper.*
- *You should glue the frame elements to the top of the lid, but it is not necessary to apply glue to items under the frame.*

Materials

- *Frame Box paper elements*
- *Scissors and/or X-Acto knife*
- *Paste or glue stick*
- *Brush for applying paste*
- *Ruler or other straightedge*
- *Scoring tool (such as a letter opener)*

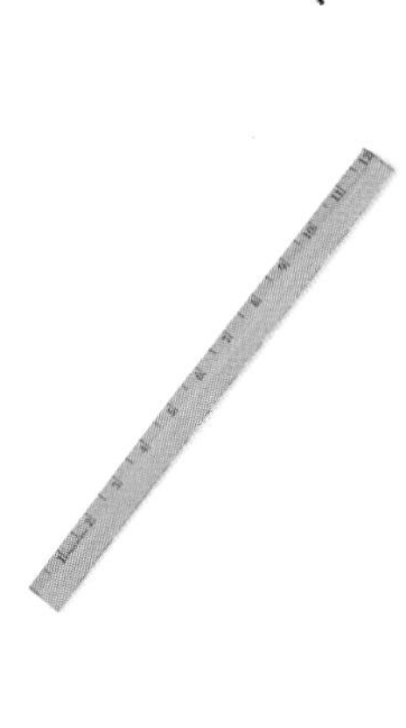

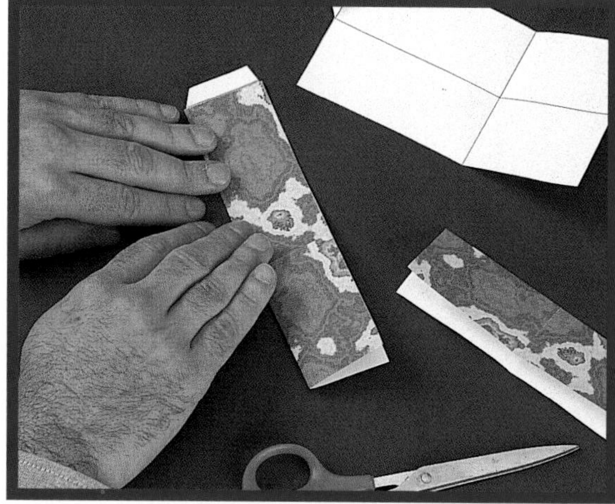

1 Valley-fold the short lines of the base wall; then carefully align the opposing long edges and fold in half so that the colored side of the paper shows. Repeat with the other base wall element. Make the folded edges sharp and clean by running the side of your thumbnail along the folded paper.

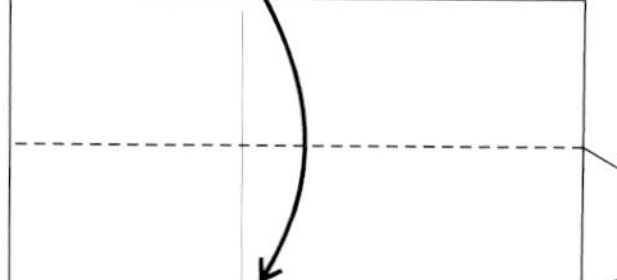

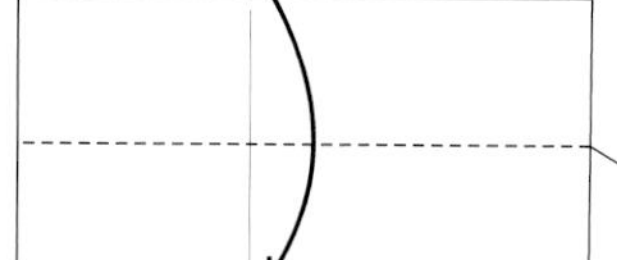

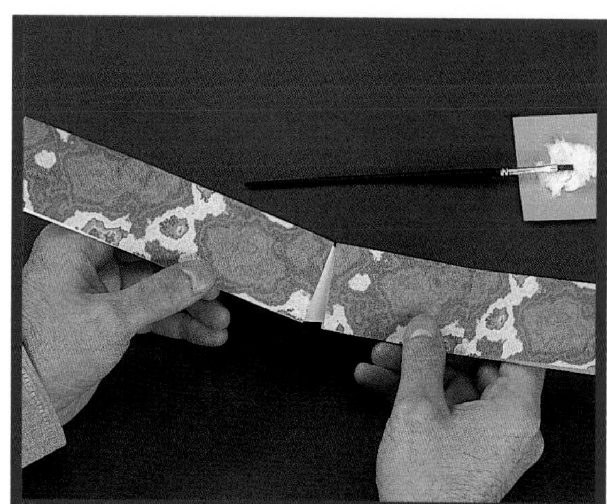

2 Apply paste to the outside of one of the tabs. The outside of a tab is on the same side as the colored side of the paper. Connect the two base wall elements together, end to end, by inserting the pasted tab of one between the folded layers of the other. The pasted tab should adhere to only one inside surface of the base wall element.

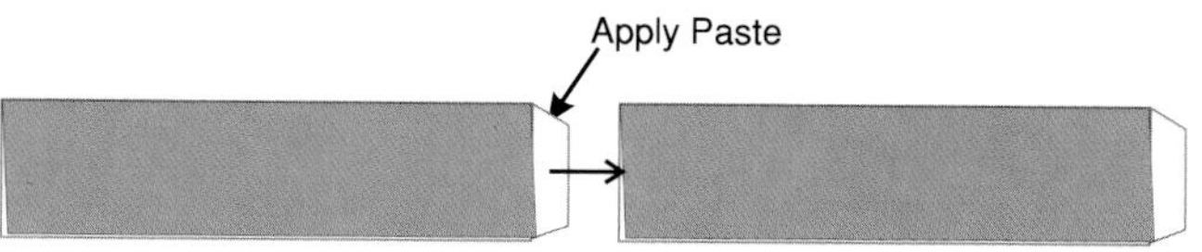

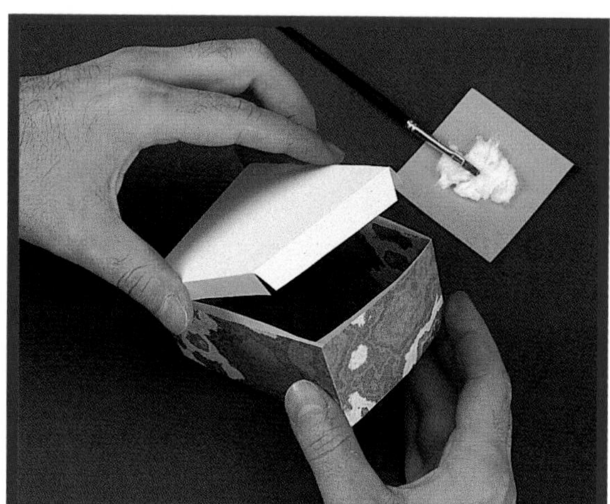

3 Apply paste to the outside of the remaining exposed tab and bring the two short ends of the base wall element together. Tuck the pasted tab between the folded layers of the end of the paper and press firmly to make a good fit. Make the rectangle even by adjusting the segment creases. You now have the base wall of the box. The top edge is folded, and the bottom of the rectangle is an open, double edge of paper. The tabs of the floor of the box will be pasted between these open edges of paper.

Prepare the floor of the box by folding the tabs to stand vertically around the edge. Apply paste to both sides of each tab. Carefully fit the tabs into the bottom, open edges of the base wall.

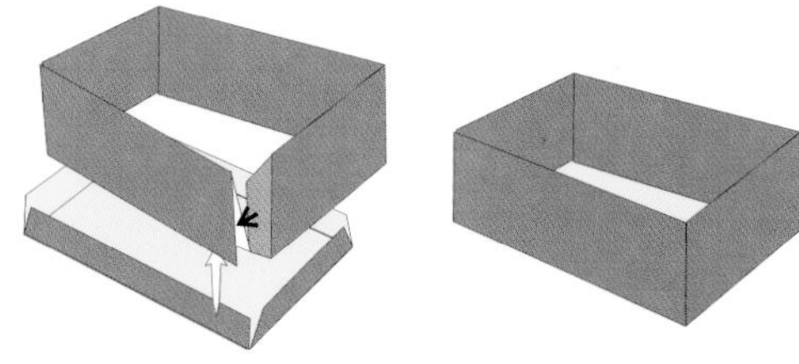

4 Fold the edges of the lid. Begin with the underside and valley-fold the innermost creases. Unfold and turn the paper over. Make the valley-folds indicated and crease them to close at right angles. Apply paste to each tab.

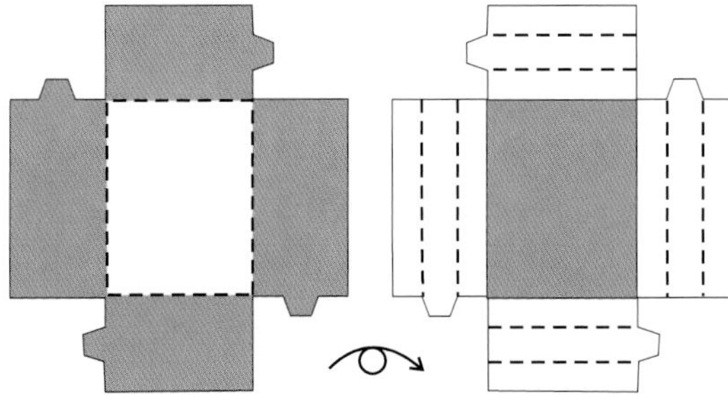

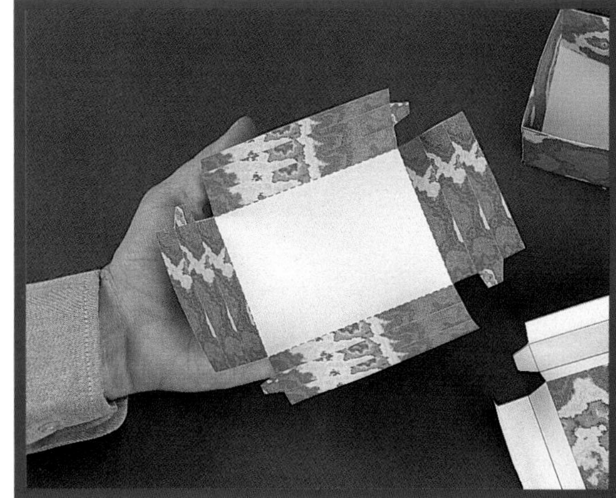

5 Tuck each pasted tab into its adjacent open lid-wall edge. Press firmly to seal. Allow lid to dry on the box base.

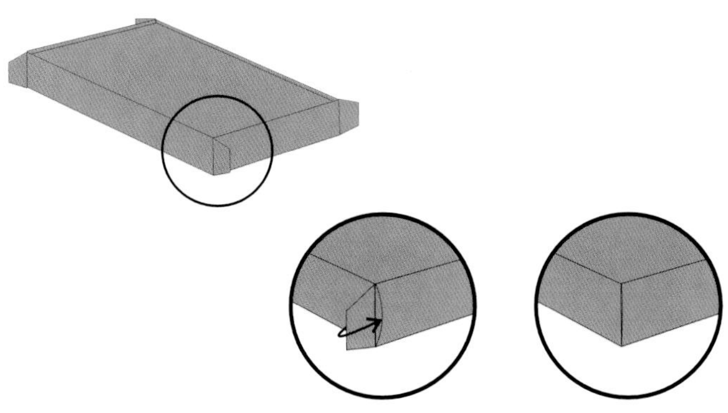

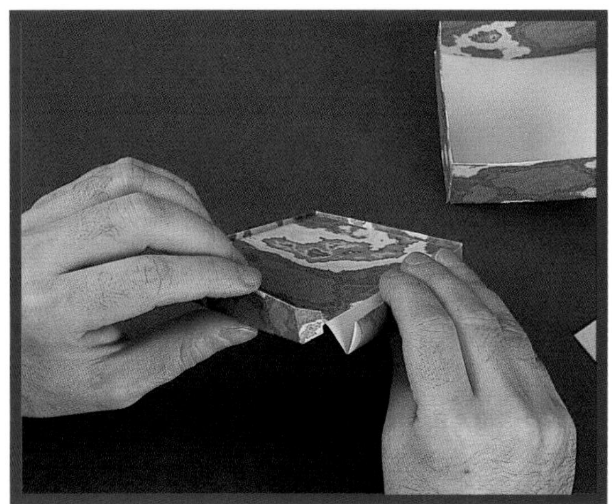

6 With an X-Acto knife, cut out the rectangular center, indicated by the innermost dotted line, then cut on the four angled, dotted lines (a). This opens the center of the frame. Valley-fold the cut edges outward and the tab edges inward (b). Turn the frame over and set the tab edges at right-angles to the face of the frame (c).

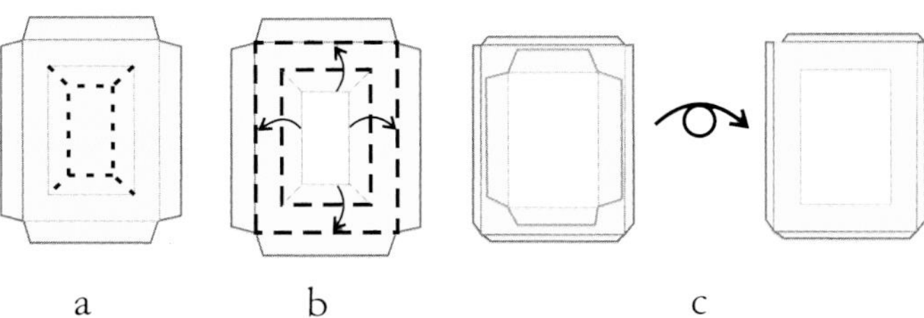

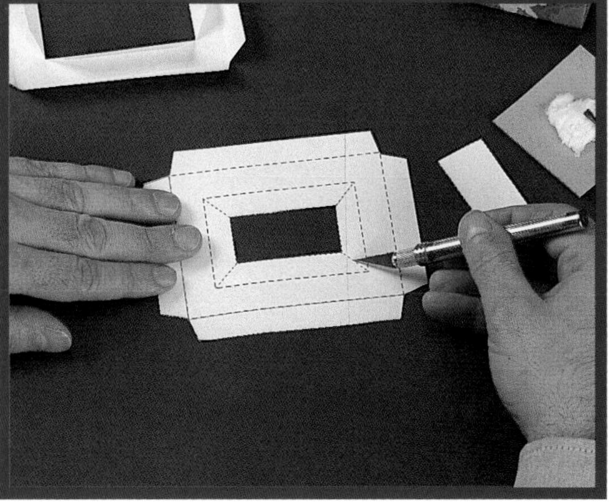

7 Insert the frame tabs into the open edges at the perimeter of the box lid. You may use glue or paste for permanence.

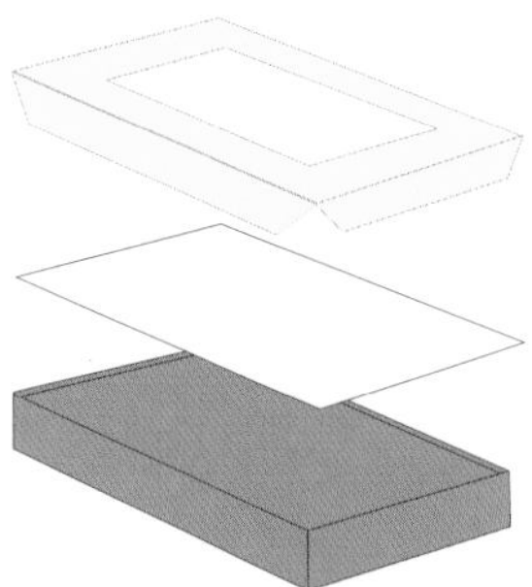

8 A photo or decorative paper may be placed between the lid and the frame before assembly. You may also experiment with other shapes for the cutout center of the frame element.

9 The finished frame box. This example shows off the colorful box paper.

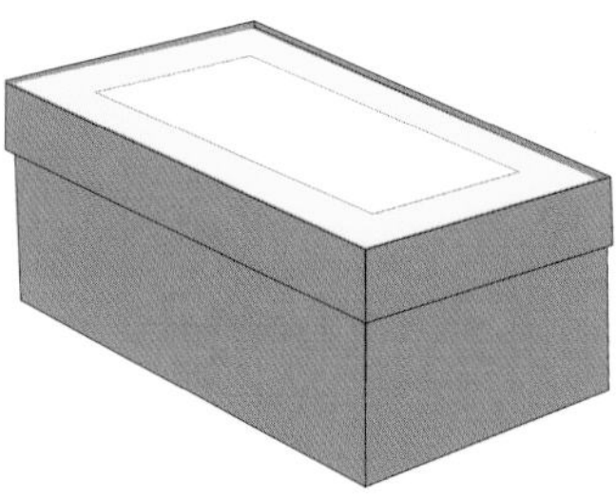

Frame Box Gallery

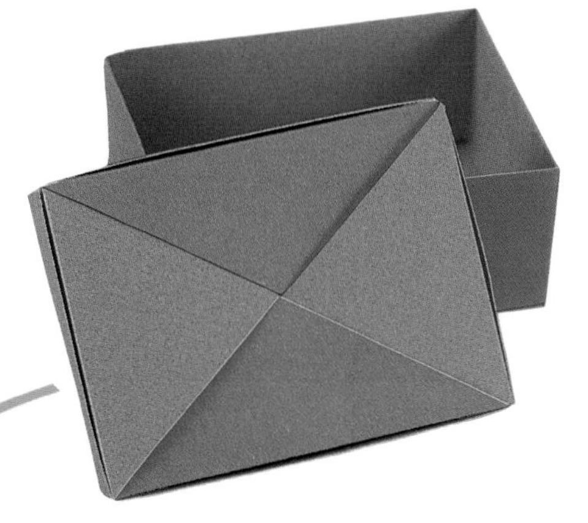

A photograph inserted in this handsome box gives added meaning to a gift, especially if it reflects the contents of the box.

Any design that fits on the cube box lid can be adapted to the frame box lid. Here, we have borrowed the woven triangle pattern.

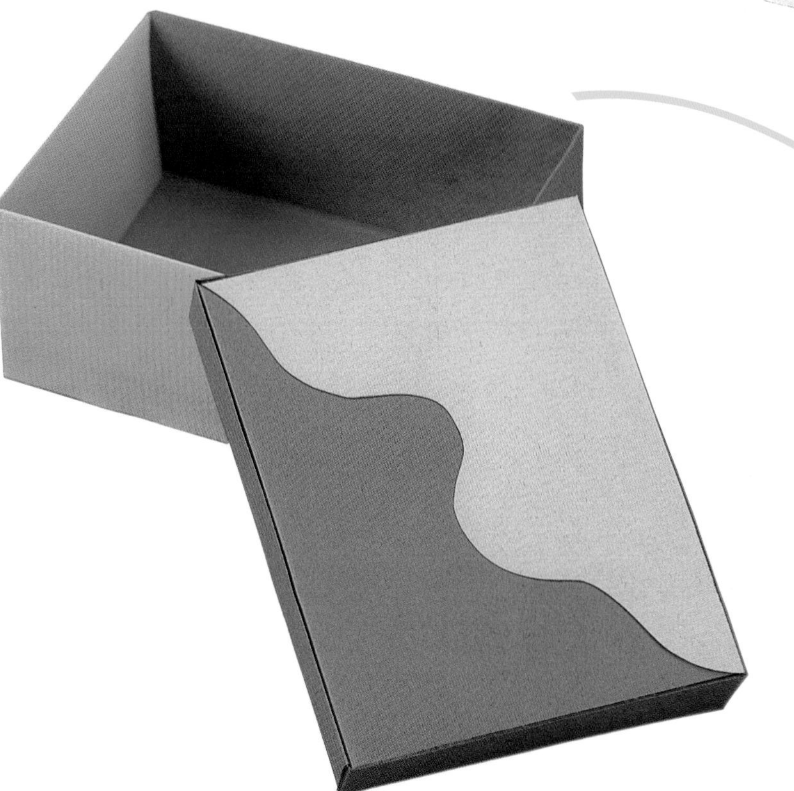

Create amusing and colorful boxes by cutting out shaped insert elements and arranging them in various ways. You can use decorative lid ideas from any of the other projects in this book.

Magician's Box

How to Build a Magician's Box

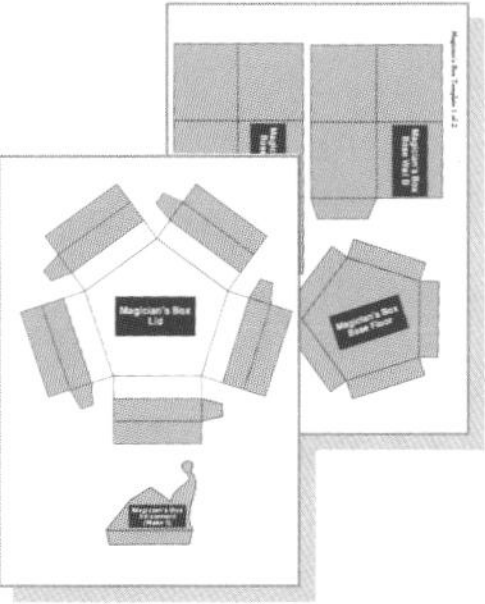

This unusual box is very versatile, and its shape is intriguing even without decoration. Children love the paper crown and mysterious-looking cutout on the lid. Metallic papers add more "magic" to this box; try foil gift wraps or even kitchen foil. To make lightweight foils sturdier, paste a sheet of paper and attach it as a backing. Changing the circle elements will change the "theme" of the magician's box: moons, stars, hearts, and diamond shapes all work well. Sure to be one of your favorite folded boxes, the magician's box may even become your personal gift-giving hallmark.

Magician's Box Tips

- *Use an X-Acto knife to cut out the curved details of the decorative lid elements. You may change the shape of the circles, which are at the end of each lid element, or make them larger or smaller.*
- *Trace the base wall elements end-to-end on a long piece of paper. This way you will have one less glued joint for the box base.*
- *You may find it desirable to trim the base floor tabs at a sharper angle before assembly. This is an especially good idea when working with lightweight paper.*

Materials

- *Magician's Box paper elements*
- *Scissors and/or X-Acto knife*
- *Paste or glue stick*
- *Brush for applying paste*

1 Valley-fold the short lines of the base wall; then carefully align the opposing long edges and fold in half so that the colored side of the paper shows. Repeat with the other base wall element. Make the folded edges sharp and clean by running the side of your thumbnail along the folded paper.

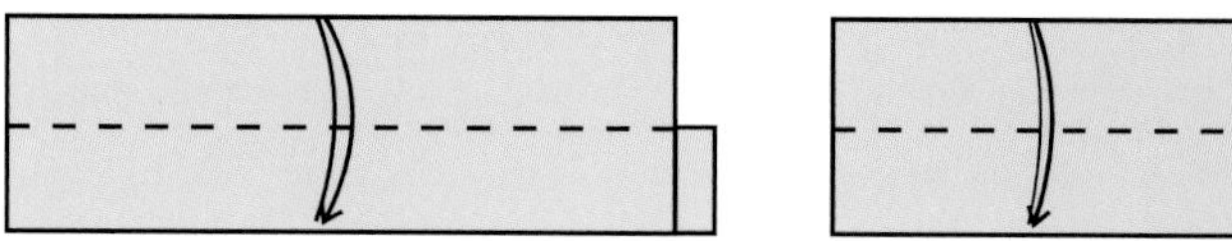

2 Apply paste to the outside of one of the tabs. The outside of a tab is on the same side as the colored side of the paper. Connect the two base wall elements together, end to end, by inserting the pasted tab of one between the folded layers of the other. The pasted tab should stick to only one inside surface of the base wall element.

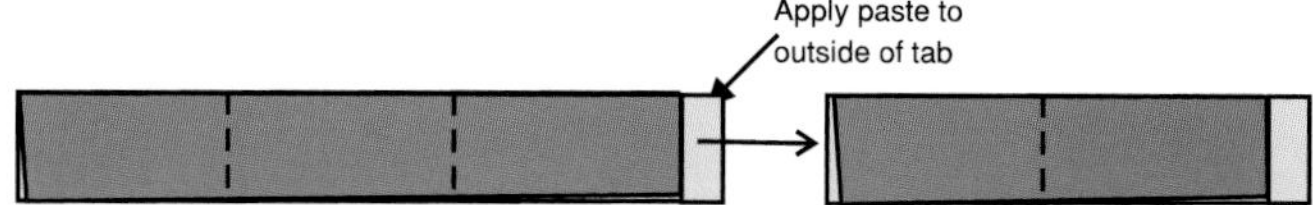

3 Apply paste to the outside of the exposed tab and bring the two ends of the base wall element together. Tuck the pasted tab between the folded layers of the end of the paper and press firmly to make a good fit.

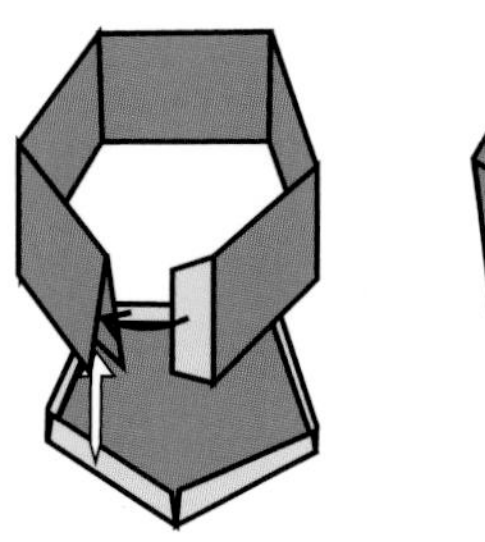

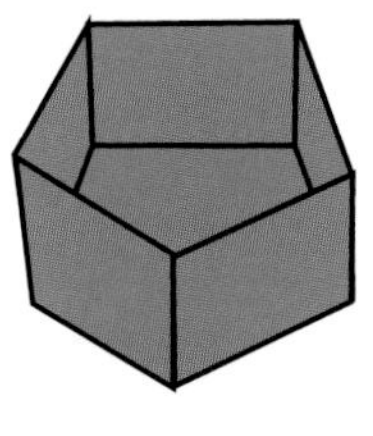

4 Make the shape even by adjusting the segment creases. You now have the base wall of the box. The top edge is folded, the bottom is an open, double edge of paper. The tabs of the floor of the box will be pasted between the open edges of paper.

Prepare the floor of the box by folding the tabs to stand vertically around the edge. Apply paste to both sides of each tab. Carefully fit the tabs into the bottom, open edges of the base wall.

5 Carefully fold the edges of the lid. Begin with the underside and valley-fold the innermost creases. Unfold and turn the paper over. Make the valley-folds indicated and crease them to close at right angles to the top of the lid. Apply paste to each tab.

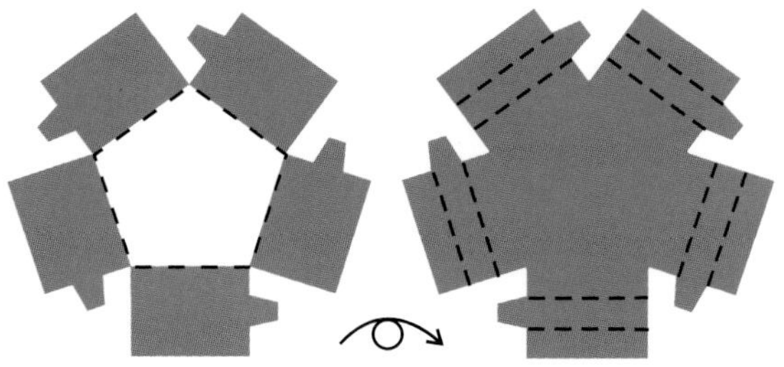

6 Tuck each pasted tab into its adjacent open lid-wall edge. Press firmly to seal. Allow the lid to dry on the box base.

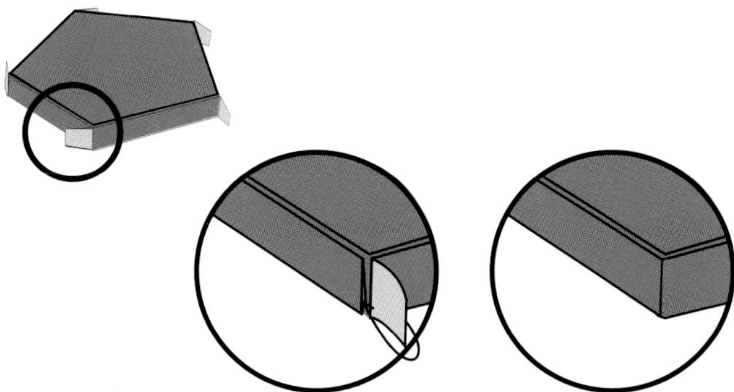

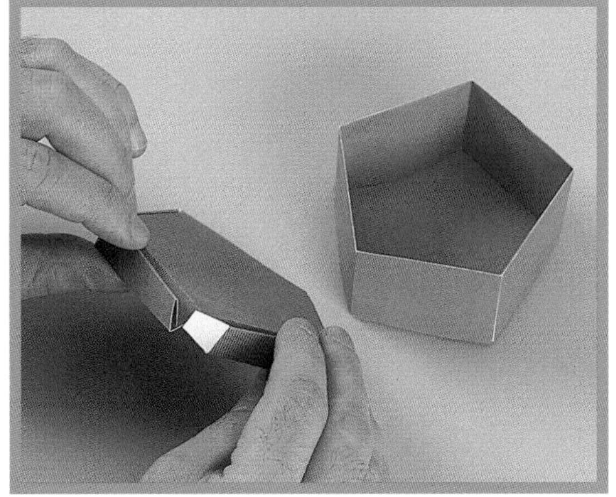

7 With a razor knife, cut out each of the five decorative lid elements. Fold sharply along the dotted line and set at an oblique angle.

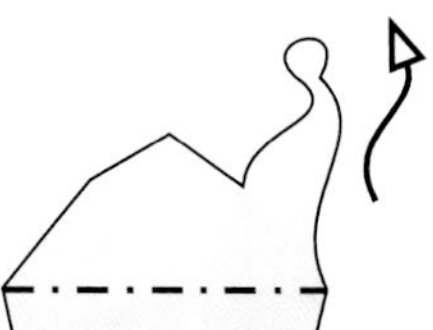

8 Insert the tab ends of the decorative elements into the open edges of the lid. Arrange them so that each element overlaps the next. Gently curve the slender extensions upward and give them a slight twist.

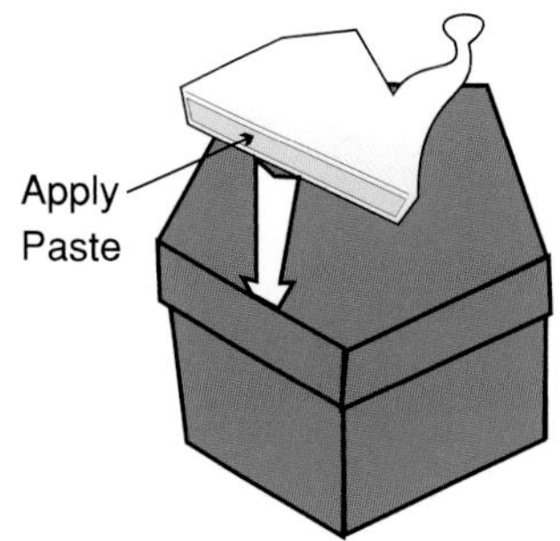

9 The finished magician's box.

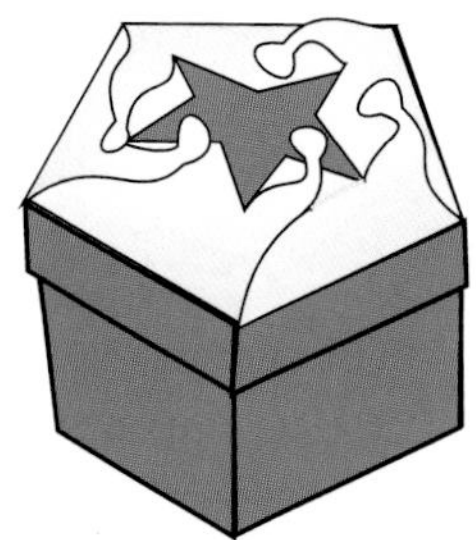

Magician's Box Gallery

Apple blossom shapes are made from the pattern and method used in the heart box project on page 40. The colors of the flowers can complement or contrast with the colors of the box.

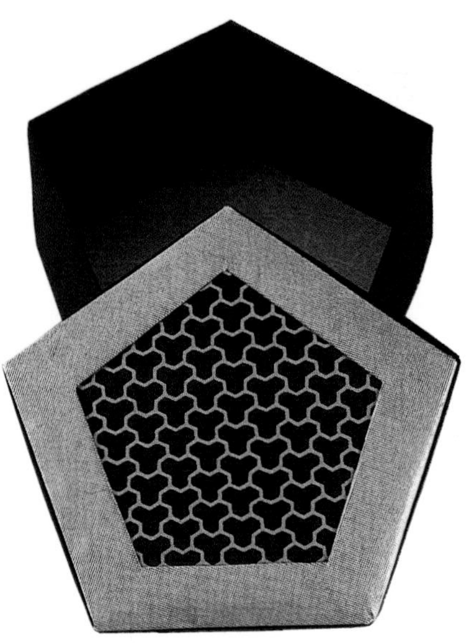

Here is an idea borrowed from the frame box project. It is elegant in black and gold: use special papers for special occasions.

Cut and layered silver foil wrapping paper adds magic to this box. Silver foil paper was pasted to the box material before the window was cut. The star cutout is framed by an overlay.

Puzzle Box

How to Build a Puzzle Box

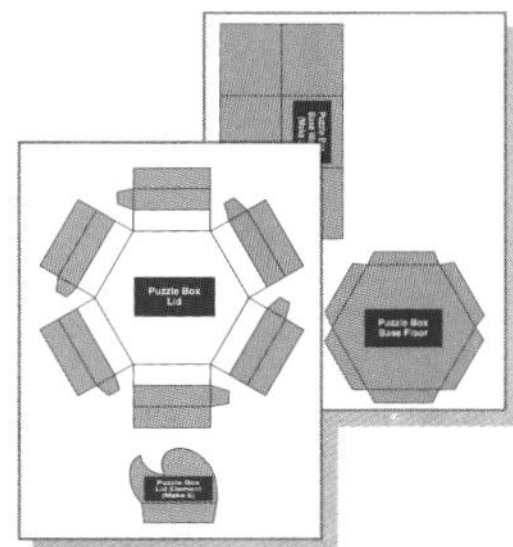

The puzzle box adds wonderful possibilities to the art of presentation. The ornamental lid segments may be created from any paper—in one, two, three or six colors. Design your own segment shapes to create an infinite combination of lid patterns, or omit the puzzle pieces to make a distinguished hexagonal box. Attractively patterned papers are especially suitable for making the box without the puzzle lid.

It is easy to scale these boxes to any dimensions you require, due to the simple geometry involved. The pattern is adaptable to many materials other than paper. Try using colored aluminum craft foils or paper-backed fabric. The basic shape of this box makes it very versatile indeed.

Materials

- *Puzzle Box paper elements*
- *Scissors and/or X-Acto knife*
- *Paste or glue stick*
- *Brush for applying paste*

Puzzle Box Tips

- *Use sharp scissors or a pointed razor knife with a fresh blade to cut out the paper pieces. This will give you cleaner edges and a better-looking box.*
- *When removing paper pieces, cut from the back side of the paper provided. Cut just inside the outlines.*
- *Where mountain-folds are shown in the diagram steps for folding the lid, there are valley-fold dashed lines on the other side of the paper. This way, fold lines will not show on the outside of the finished model.*
- *If you make more boxes from heavier paper, pre-crease all fold lines by scoring with a straightedge and scoring tool.*
- *Ordinary white paste, or convenient glue sticks, are preferable to liquid glues for this project. Use only the smallest amount of glue, to prevent warping.*

1 Valley-fold the short lines of the base wall; then carefully align the opposing long edges and fold in half so that the colored side of the paper shows. Repeat with the other base wall element. Make the folded edges sharp and clean by running the side of your thumbnail along the folded paper.

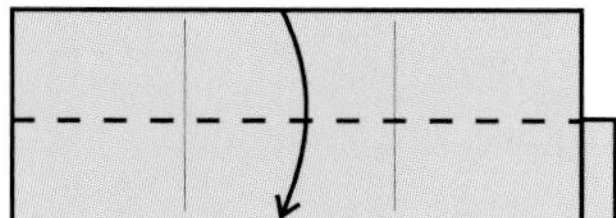

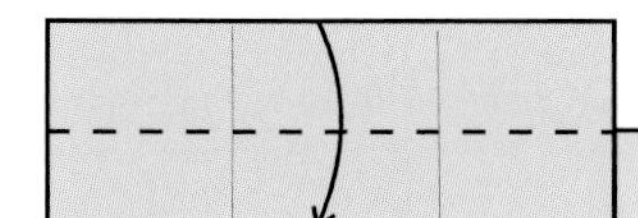

2 Apply paste to the outside of one of the tabs. The outside of a tab is on the same side as the colored side of the paper. Connect the two base wall elements together, end to end, by inserting the pasted tab of one between the folded layers of the other. The pasted tab should stick to only one inside surface of the base wall element.

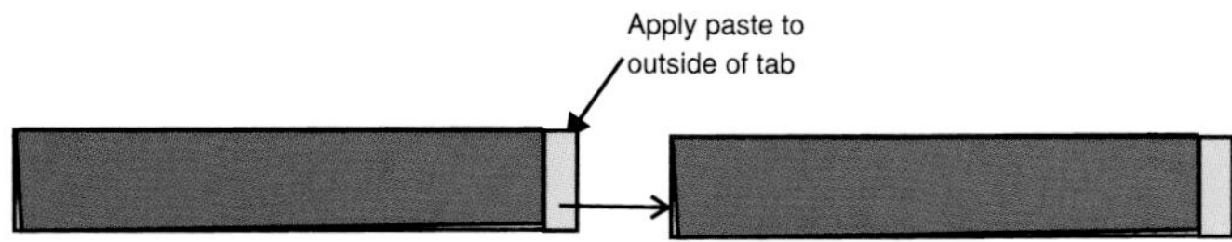

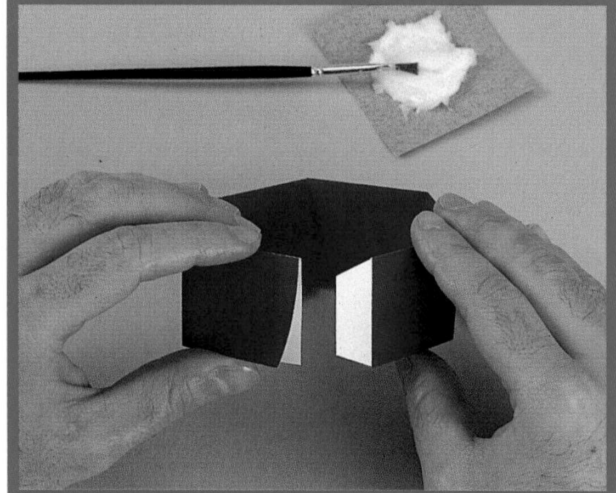

3 Apply paste to the outside of the exposed tab and bring the two ends of the base wall element together. Tuck the pasted tab between the folded layers of the end of the paper and press firmly to make a good fit.

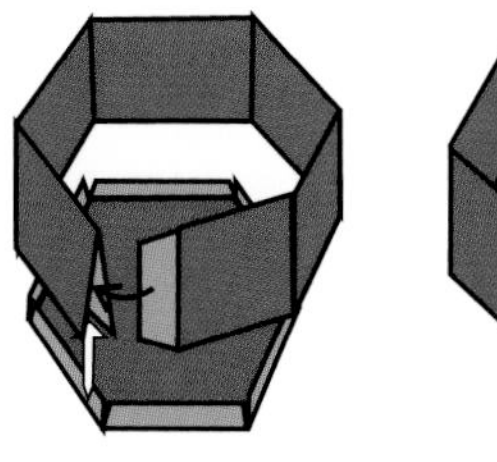

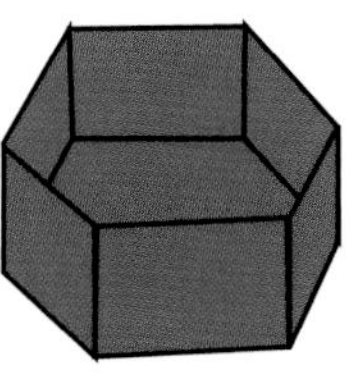

4 Sharpen and adjust the segment creases to create an evenly shaped hexagonal ring. This ring forms the walls of the base of the box. The top of the ring is a folded edge, and the bottom of the ring is an open, double edge of paper. The tabs of the floor of the box are pasted between these open edges of paper.

Prepare the floor of the box by folding the tabs to stand vertically around the hexagonal edge of the piece. Apply paste to both sides of each tab. Carefully fit the tabs into the bottom, open edges of the base wall assembly.

5 Carefully fold the edges of the lid. Begin with the underside and valley-fold the innermost creases. Unfold and turn the paper over. Make the valley-folds indicated and crease them to close at right angles to the top of the lid. You should now have a lid with a blue top and yellow sides.

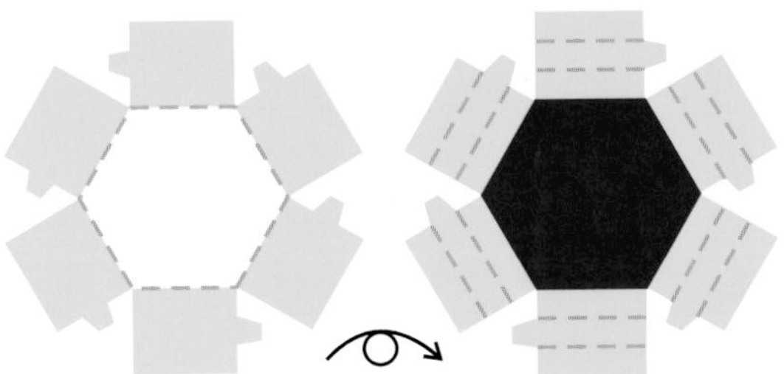

6 Apply paste to the tabs, and tuck each pasted tab into its adjacent open lid-wall edge. Press firmly to seal. Allow the lid to dry on the box base.

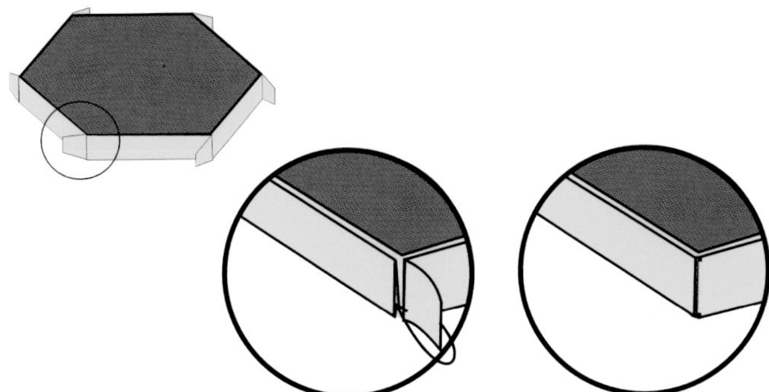

7 Fold the tab edge of each of the six puzzle elements. Make this fold very sharp and clean.

8 Insert the tab ends of the puzzle elements into the edges of the box lid. Alternate the colors and make sure that the pointed end of each shape is visible. The result will be a wonderful pattern. You can experiment with other ways to arrange the papers in the lid, or design other shapes of your own.

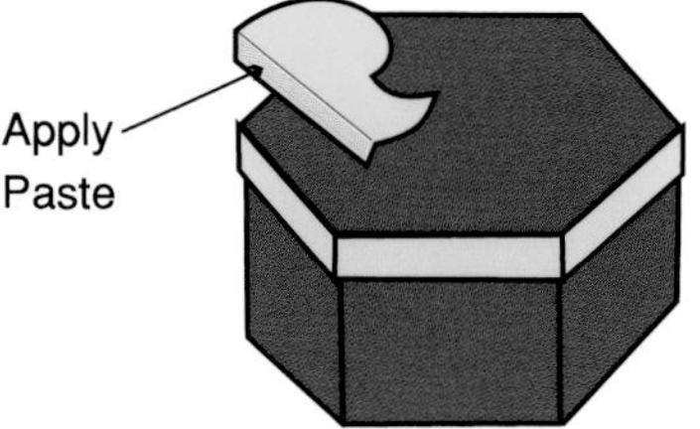

9 The finished puzzle box.

Puzzle Box Gallery

You can keep the construction simple by using ornate papers or get fancy by applying delicate cutout shapes to make these decorative flower themes.

There are endless possibilities with modular lid elements. Some element shapes can be installed in more than one way. The even number of box sides allows for many color possibilities.

Here are coordinated desktop accessories: a pencil holder and a paper clip box. The pencil holder can be weighted with uncooked rice or dried beans to prevent tipping and support pencils in the cup.

Heart Box

How to Build a Heart Box

A gift to the one you love is even more thoughtful and personal when presented in this handmade token of affection. But don't wait until Valentine's Day to transform your favorite paper into a lovely keepsake with this heart box pattern.

From cutting to final assembly, this project can be completed in less than half an hour. The heart-shaped top of the lid may be decorated as simply or elaborately as desired, or not at all. Rubber stamps, cutouts, colorful stickers, and colored markers can all be employed to personalize this classic gift box.

Heart Box Tips

- *Make all of the flat folds first and organize the paper elements in groups: one for the lid and one for the base. This is especially important for this project, since the box lid and floor look the same and are only slightly different in size.*
- *Use the edge of a table or a ruler to curve rounded elements. Do so in a gentle way with several passes. Heavy-handed curling will cause the edges to become misaligned.*
- *Apply glue a few dabs at a time when going around curves. You will have better control and will be less likely to get glue on the visible surfaces of your project.*
- *Use a white craft glue to attach the flowers to the lid of the box. Use paste to assemble the tab elements.*

Materials

- *Heart Box paper elements*
- *Scissors and/or X-Acto knife*
- *Paste or glue stick*
- *White craft glue*
- *Brush for applying paste*

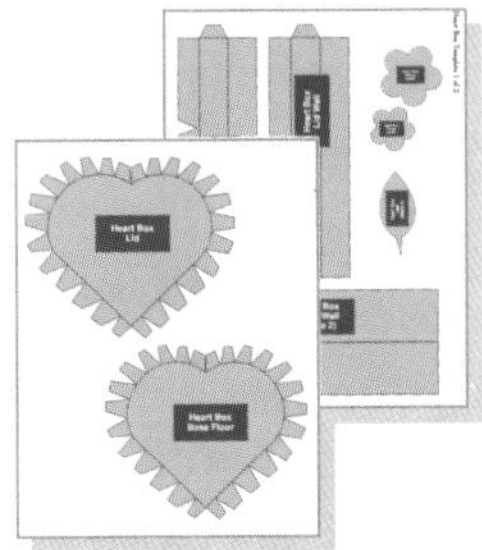

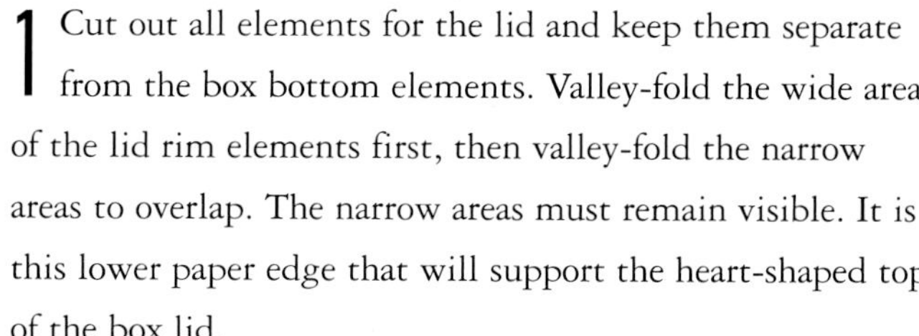

1 Cut out all elements for the lid and keep them separate from the box bottom elements. Valley-fold the wide area of the lid rim elements first, then valley-fold the narrow areas to overlap. The narrow areas must remain visible. It is this lower paper edge that will support the heart-shaped top of the box lid.

Valley-fold the tabs of the heart-shaped lid. Turn the lid over so that the tabs point downward.

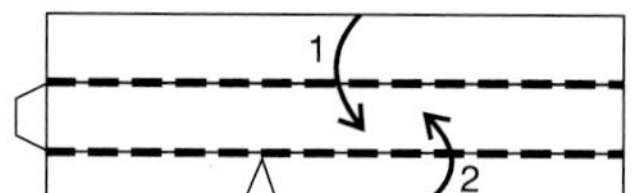

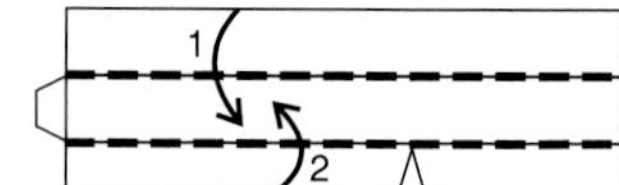

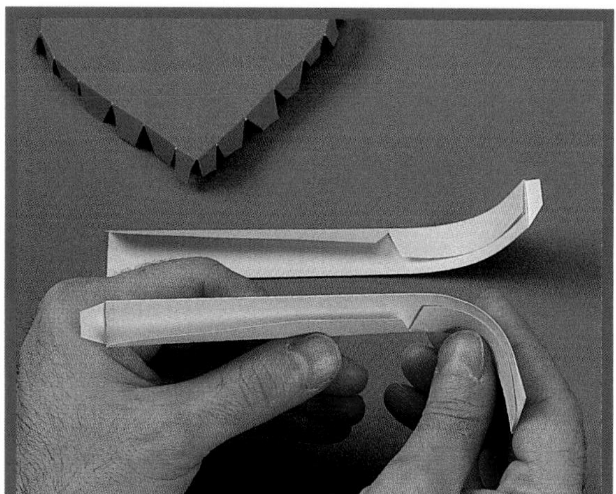

2 Each lid-rim paper has a V-notch that divides its length. Gently curve the short end of each lid rim paper. Keep the notch on the inside of the curve.

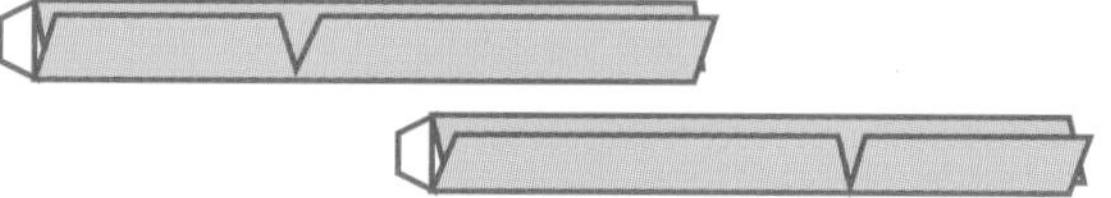

3 Apply paste to both sides of the tabs of the lid top paper. You may paste and tuck as you go along. Assemble the lid by inserting the tabs of the heart-shaped top into the open edges of the rim papers. Tuck the end tab of each rim into the open ends of the other rim.

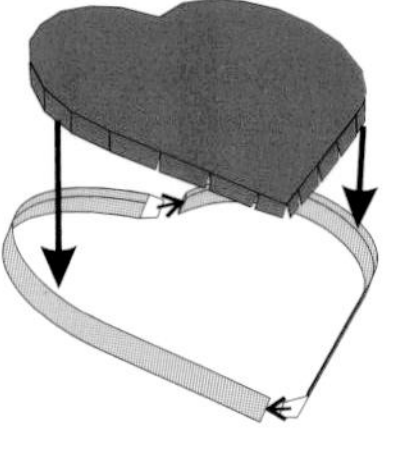

4 Valley-fold the base rim elements and the tabs of the base floor.

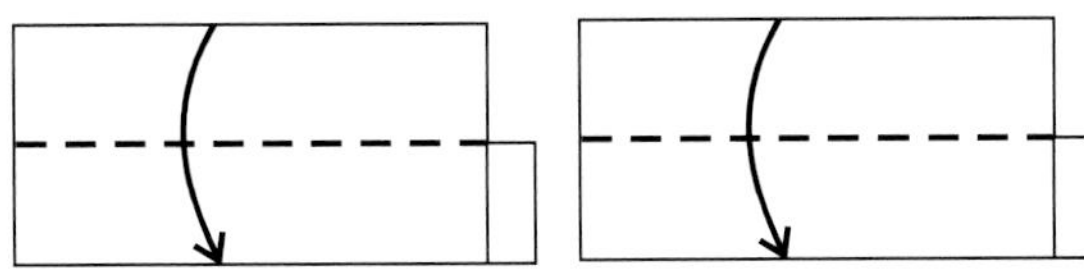

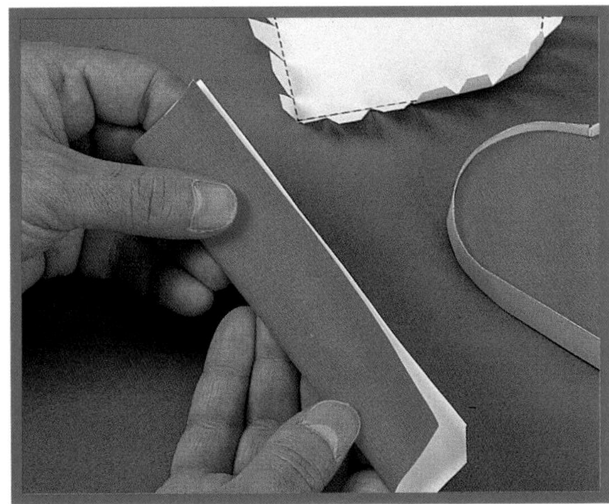

5 Gently curve one end of each of the base walls, then apply paste to both sides of the tabs of the base floor paper. Assemble the base by inserting the tabs of the heart-shaped floor between the open edges of the base wall papers. Tuck the end tab of each rim into the open end of the other rim.

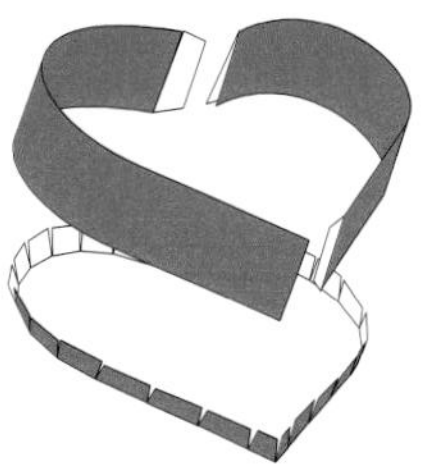

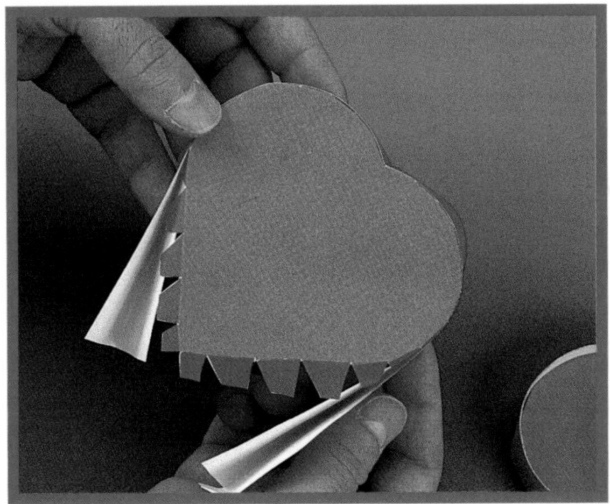

6 Shape the leaves by first folding them in half lengthwise, then tightly fan-folding them from one end to the other. Open the leaf out and shape it.

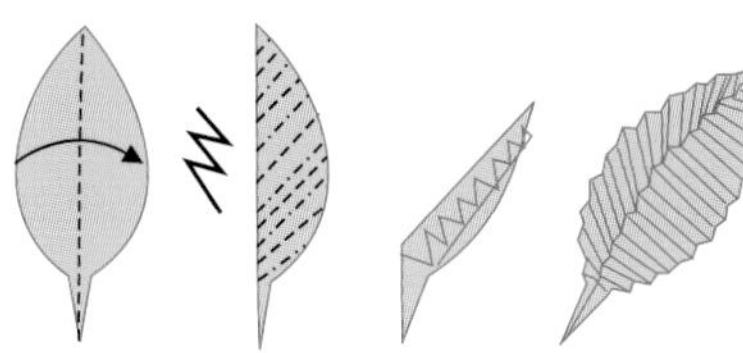

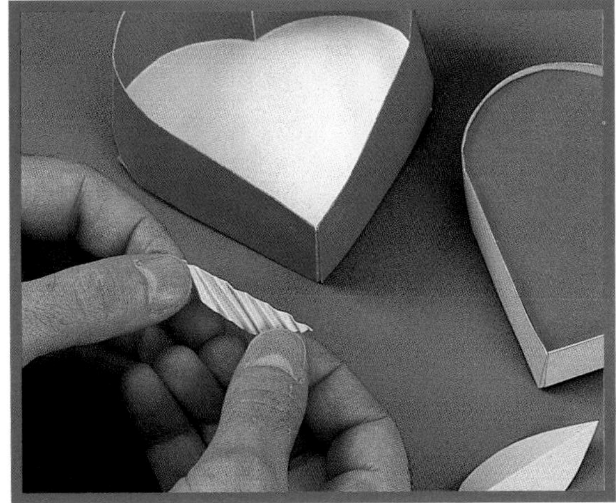

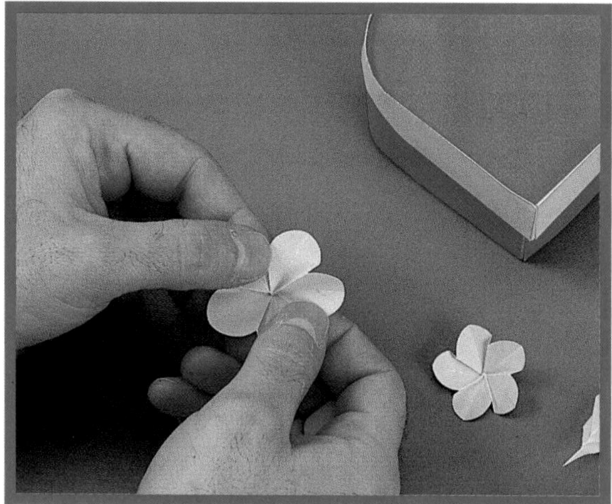

7 Shape the blossoms by mountain- and valley-folding them between each of the five petals, in a radial pattern from the center. Gently curl each petal for a softer shape. Glue the smaller petal set into the center of the larger one.

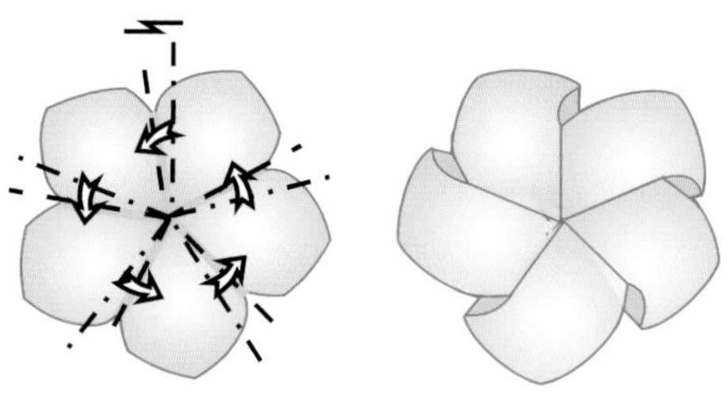

8 Arrange and assemble the leaves and the blossom. Secure them with glue.

9 The finished heart box.

Heart Box Gallery

The heart box may be adorned with a simple bow. This package bow was adapted from the lotus box lid ornament and folded from gold foil gift wrap.

Pierced patterns are very effective on heart lids. Trace a pattern on the back of the lid and cut it out with an X-Acto knife. Back the pierced pattern with white or a contrasting color of paper.

The classic Valentine's Day presentation, filled with tempting sweets.

Lotus Box

How to Build a Lotus Box

The lotus symbolizes creation, and this lotus can be created anywhere there is paper. An ideal project to teach to children who can then teach their friends! This origami box requires no glue or scissors to make: It is folded from square paper. To make paper square, simply fold the short edge of any paper rectangle against the long edge, forming a triangle with a rectangular remnant along one edge. Trim away the remnant and unfold the paper. You now have a square sheet of paper. Easy to do anywhere, use lightweight paper for best results.

Materials

- *Two sheets of eight-inch square paper, one green and one yellow*
- *One seven and one half-inch sheet of green paper*

Lotus Box Tips

- *Be sure that the papers are cut perfectly square and to the proper size.*
- *Sharpen all creases with the side of your thumbnail to make them look neat and help them keep their shape longer.*
- *Cut up colorful old magazines for material. The weight and size of magazine paper is ideal for this project.*

1 The folding of the lid and the base are identical. The base paper is one-eighth smaller than the lid paper, so it will fit inside the finished lid. Begin with the largest green paper—with the white side up. (a) Valley-fold paper in half, corner to corner, both ways. Unfold the paper to see that the two fold lines will cross in the middle of the square.

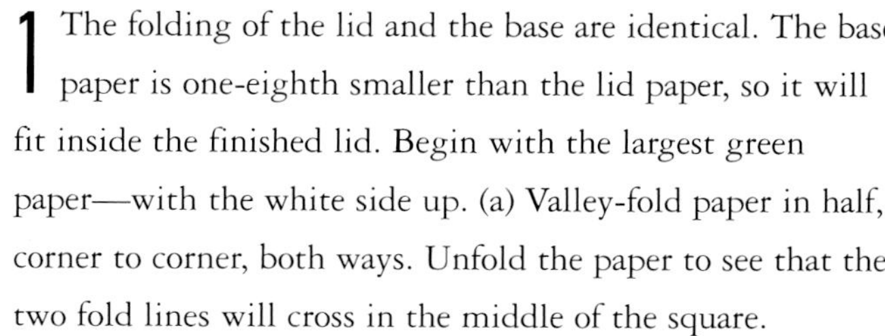

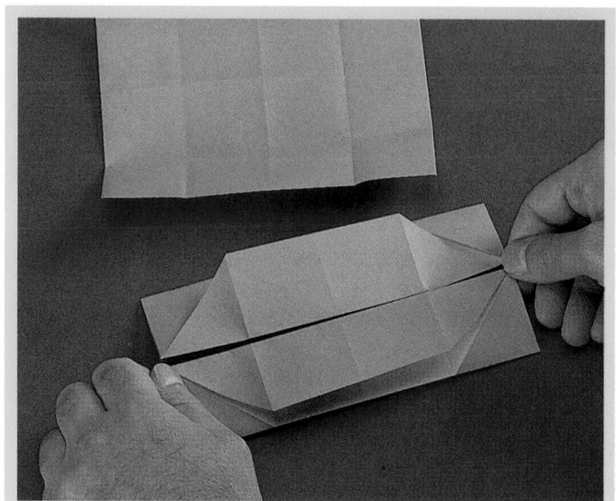

2 (b) Valley-fold the four corners to the center of the square. Unfold the paper. (c) Valley-fold the four corners of the square to the center of the fold lines created in the previous step. (d) Valley-fold the green folded edges in, along the crease lines already made. (e) The models will now look like the illustration shown. Turn the models over. (f) (magnification) Valley-fold the opposite side edges to the vertical center line of the square. Unfold.

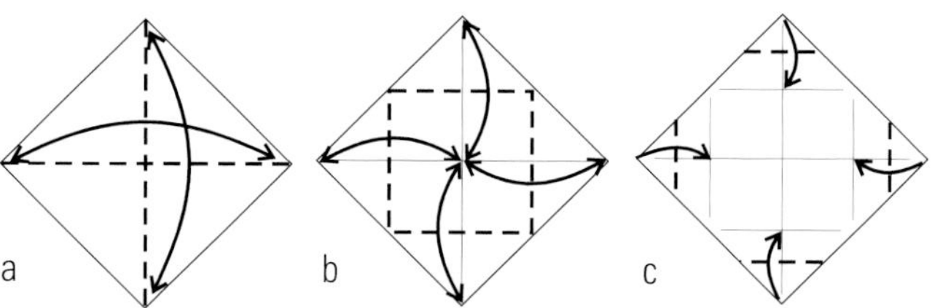

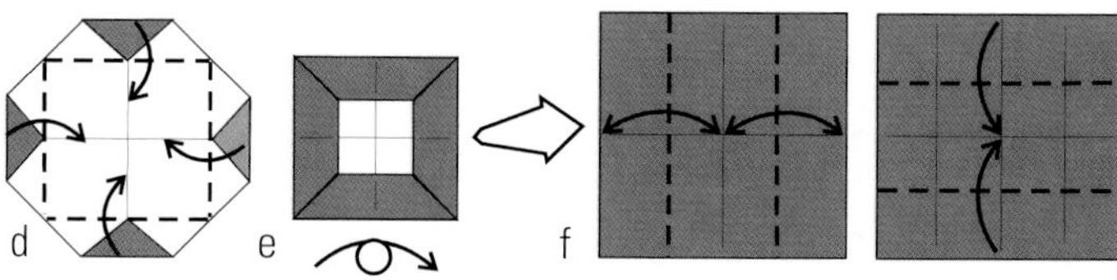

3 (g) Valley-fold the top and bottom edges to the horizontal center line. (h) Flip up the lower flap to the top of the model to reveal the white side of the paper. (i) Valley-fold the lower green corners to the square angled crease lines. (j) Return the flap to its original position. Repeat steps g, h, and i on the other side of the paper.

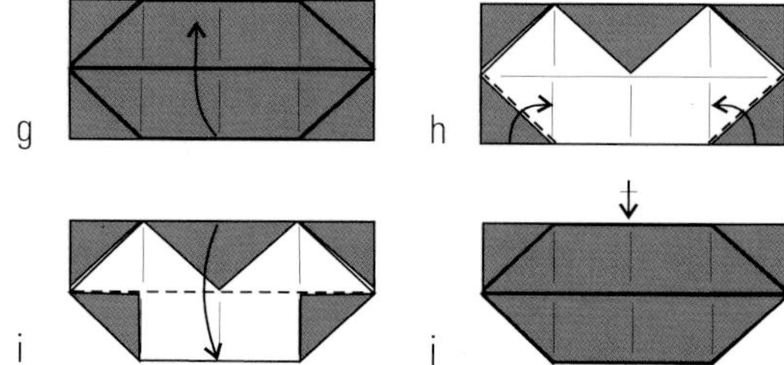

4 (k) The model should now look like this. Open the model from the center. (l) Push in the corners and square the four box walls. (m) Follow steps a-l to fold the smaller green paper (for the lid). Both the lid and the base should match the drawing and one should fit inside the other.

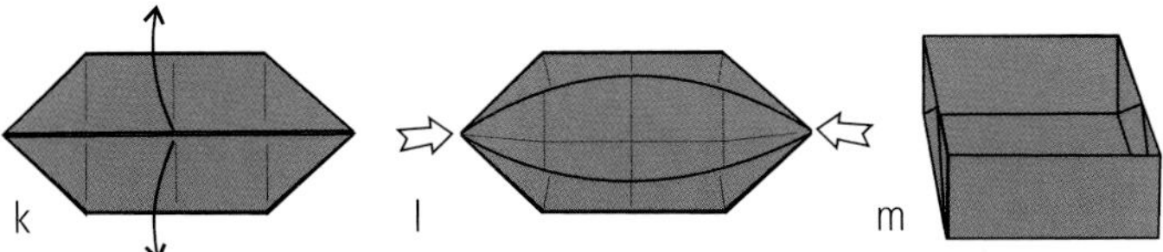

5 Use the yellow square for the lotus top. (a) Begin with the white side up. Fold the square in half, edge to edge, both ways. (b) Unfold to reveal the white paper again. (c) Fold the four corners of the square to the center of the paper. (d) Fold the four new corners to the center. The model will look like the illustration and will have two layers of four yellow "petals" on this side.

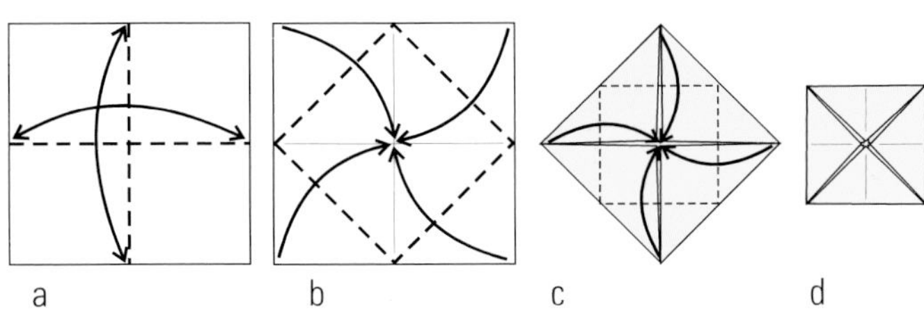

6 (e) (magnification) Fold the four petal corners of the first layer to the center of their outer edge. (f) Model will look like the illustration. (g) Fold the petal corners of the second (inner) layer to the framed corners of the model. (h) Model will look like the illustration. Turn the model over.

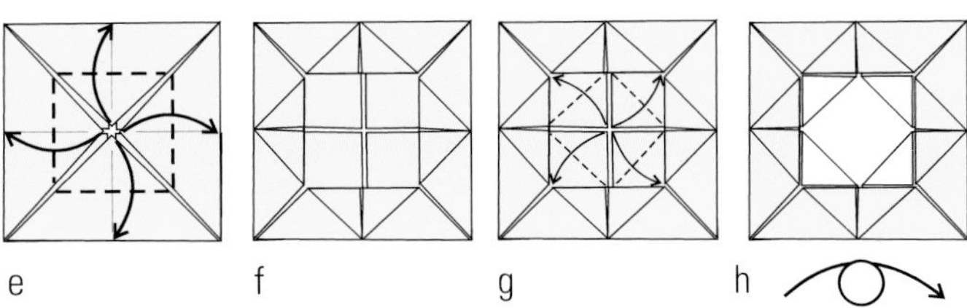

7 (i) Fold the corners of this square to the center. (j) Unfold and set at right angles to the square base. These are the base points. (k) Turn the model over. (l) Slightly elevate the eight petal points marked by dots in the drawing. This is the lotus form.

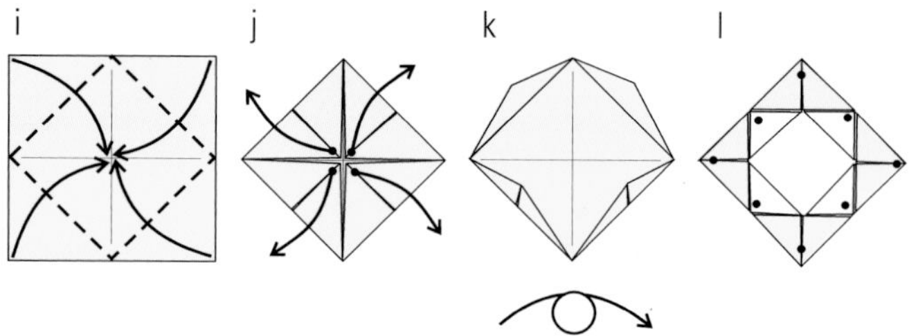

8 Insert the four base corners into the open edges of the box lid.

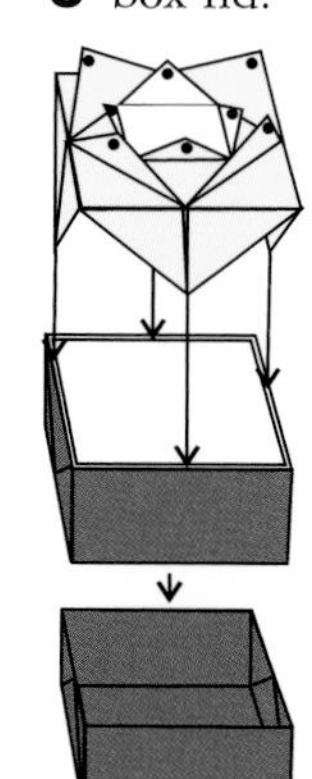

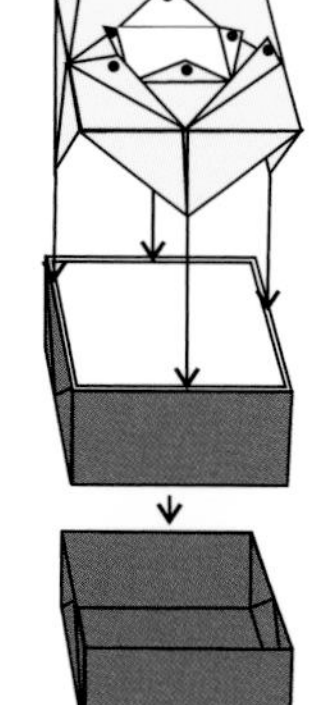

9 The finished lotus box.

Lotus Box Gallery

Here the lotus box is used as a photo frame. Unfold the lotus and insert a photo or a slip of contrasting colored paper, then re-fold with the element enclosed.

Fold several smaller lotus elements and insert them into the opening of the main lotus. You can experiment with colors and make more petals with a few scissor cuts.

Standard origami papers come in a wide variety of colors and patterns. All can be used for the lotus box.

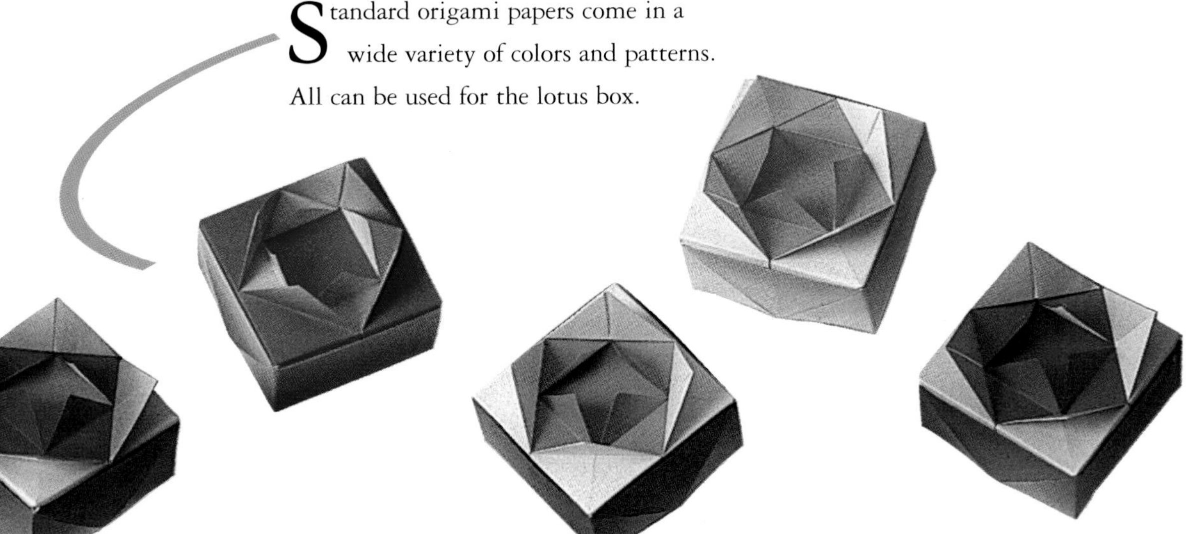

Match Box

How to Build a Match Box

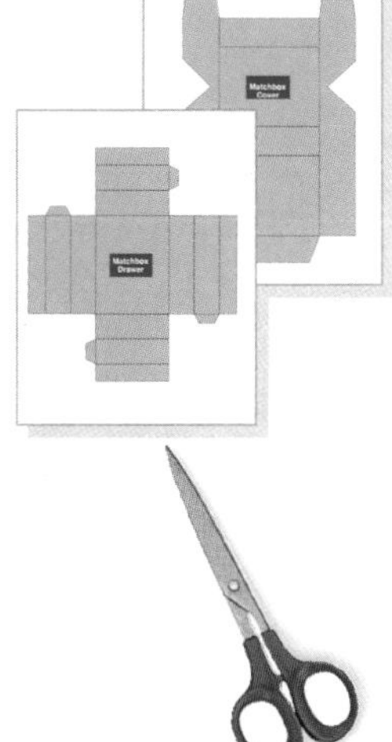

Real matchboxes are hard to come by these days. Remember how useful they were for craft projects and for storing small items? Matchboxes are still the perfect size for organizing small collections; whether sea shells, minerals, beads, or buttons. For the hobbyist, matchboxes are a great way to store and display supplies and small tools.

Although they won't be emblazoned with the name of the latest restaurant or club, making your own matchboxes has some great advantages: you don't have to get rid of any matches before you can use the box, you can customize the matchbox size to your purpose, and you can choose the color of the box. Just about any type of paper works well for this project. Colorful and pattered papers can be made into splendid boxes for small gifts. The simplicity of this design makes it easy to customize and personalize matchboxes for any occasion.

Materials

- *Match Box paper elements*
- *Scissors and/or X-Acto knife*
- *Ruler or other straightedge*
- *Paste or glue stick*
- *White craft glue*

Match Box Tips

- *Pre-score all creases for accuracy and neatness. The boxes fit together better when they are folded neatly.*
- *Use paste sparingly, and let pasted pieces dry completely before inserting the box drawer into the sliding cover. This will keep the drawer from becoming accidentally glued shut.*
- *If you want to show parallel bands on the matchbox cover, skip cutting the notches for the diamond frame. You may also cut other shapes: Circles, ovals, rectangles, etc. Experiment by changing the margin widths, too.*
- *You may alter the scale of this box to create larger containers. Use heavyweight paper for very large boxes. Try building a nesting set of several matchboxes.*

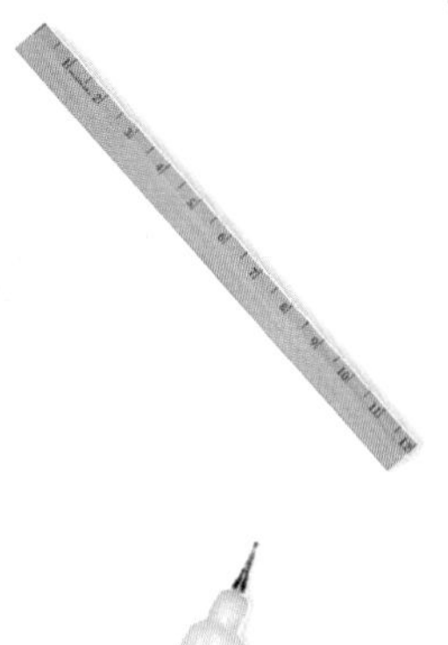

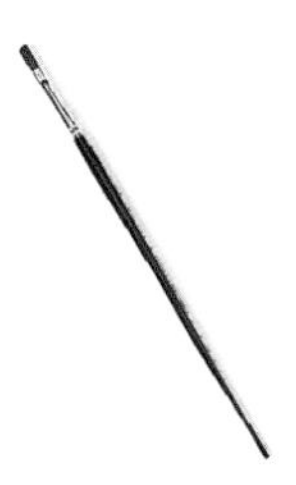

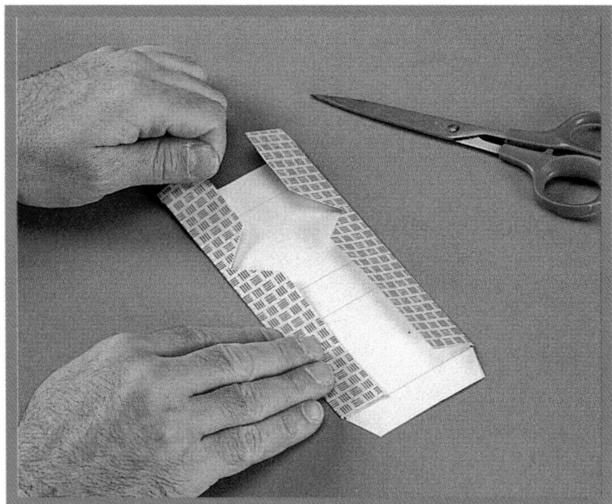

1 Make the slide cover first. Valley-fold the notched edges of the paper inward. You will notice that the notched edges form an open diamond-shape over a contrasting field of color. Turn the paper over.

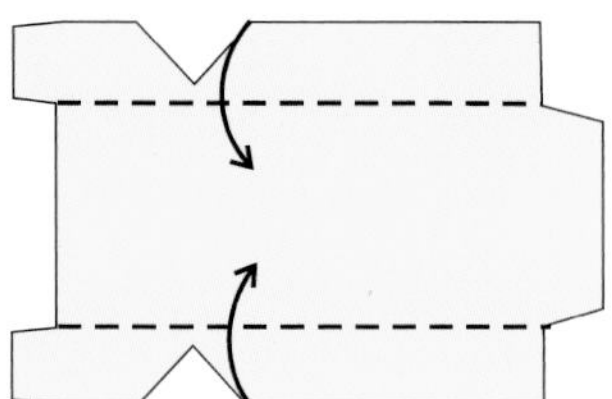

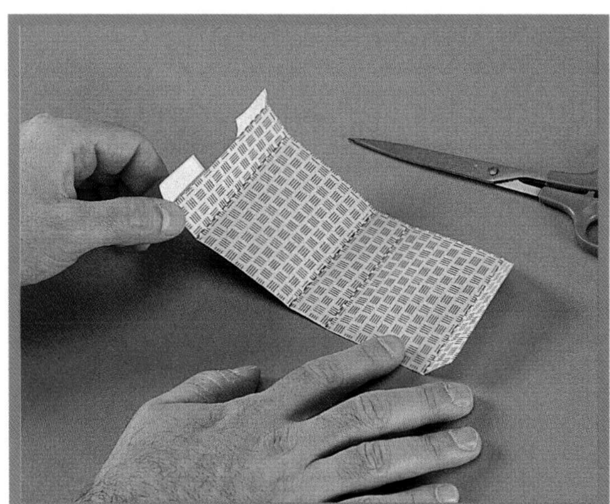

2 Valley-fold on indicated creases as shown, to form separate wall sections for the slide cover. You may wish to pre-score these valley-creases with a ruler and a ball-point pen.

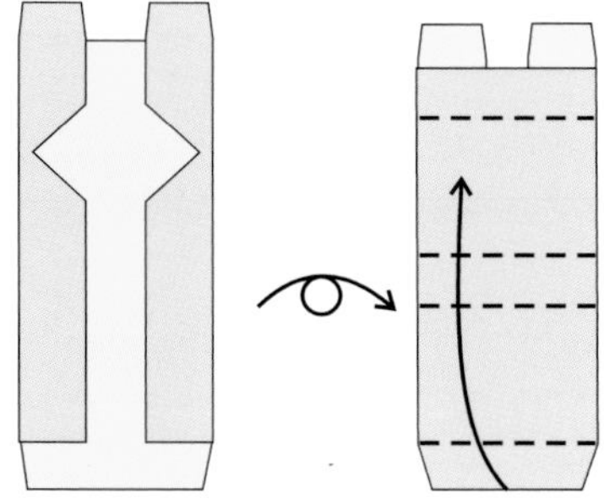

3 Tuck the single, wide tab into the opposite end of the paper form. You may use paste, but it is not necessary.

4 Tuck the two, smaller tabs under the square-ended open layers. Secure the layers with paste. Square-up the box form to evenly align the walls: make the creases neat. Turn the model over to display the diamond-framed side.

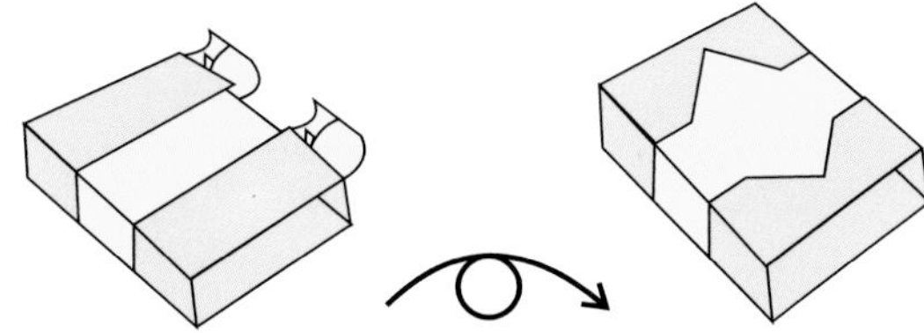

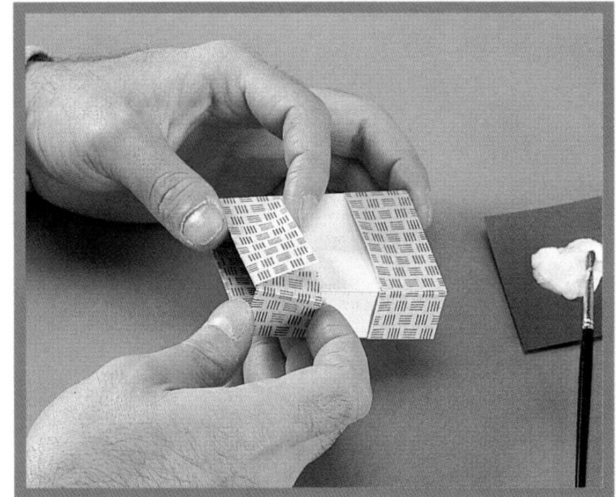

5 Valley-fold on the indicated dashed lines to create the floor of the box drawer. Turn the paper over.

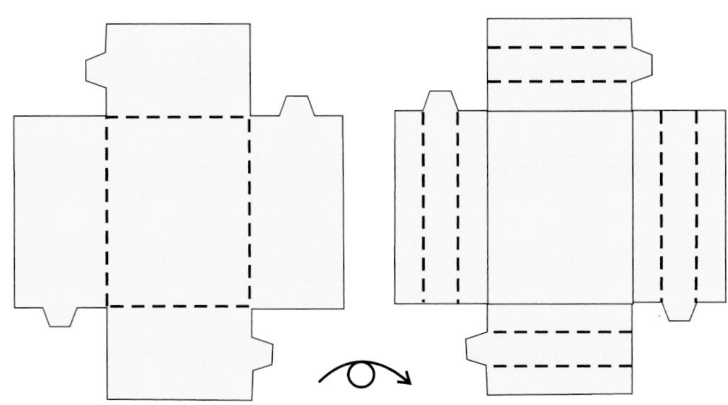

6 Valley-fold on the indicated dashed lines to make the four walls of the box drawer. On the same side of the paper, valley-fold the tabs inward.

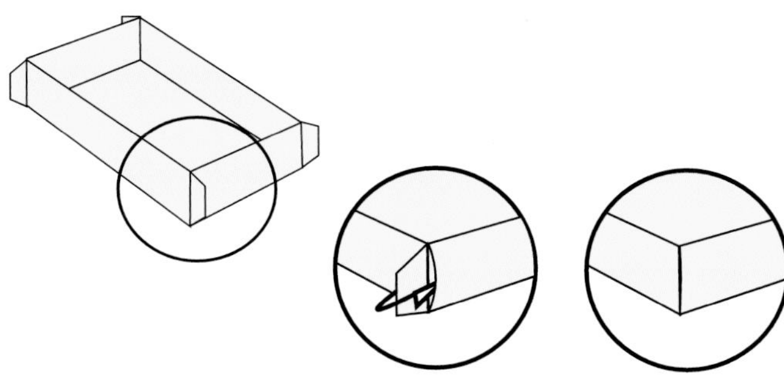

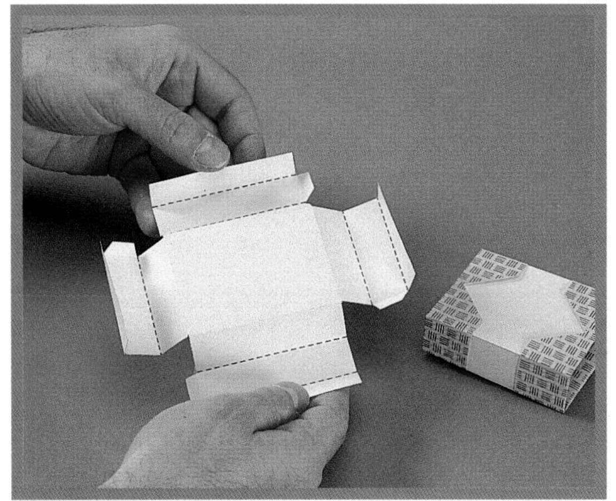

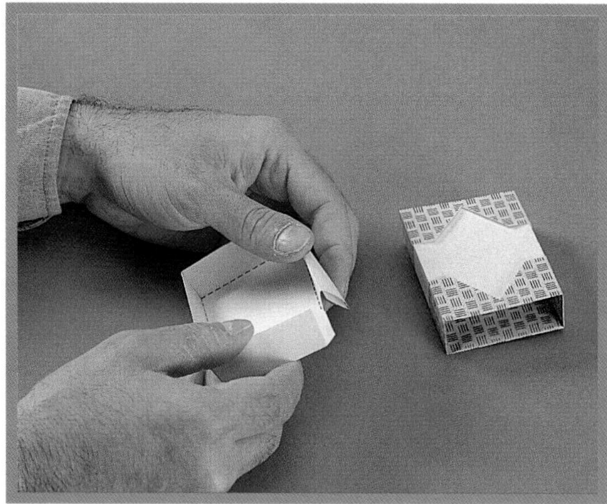

7 Fold closed the four walls of the box drawer and tuck the corner tabs into their respective corner pockets, as shown. The corner pockets are formed by the multiple layers of the box walls. Use paste to secure the corner tabs.

8 Slide the matchbox drawer into its cover.

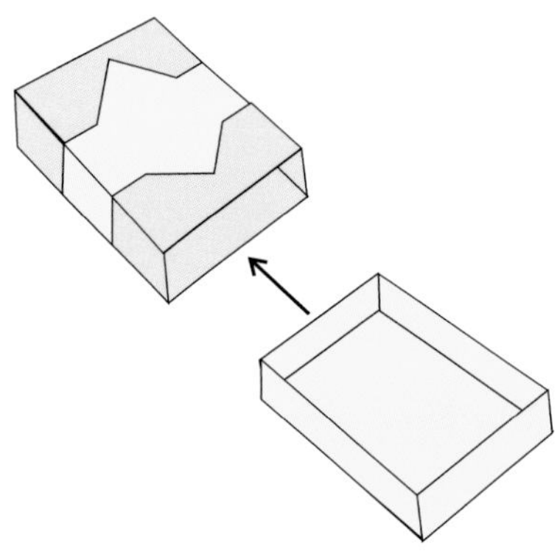

9 The finished matchbox.

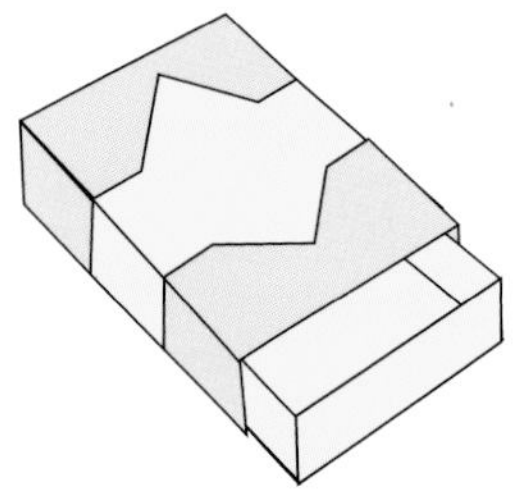

Match Box Gallery

Color-coded storage boxes are a snap with this simple box project. Insert any color or texture of paper under the folded layers of the slide cover. Makes a colorful desktop accessory.

Personalized matchboxes for gift giving. Names can be printed or handwritten on separate pieces of paper, then inserted in the open frame layer during the first few steps of the project.

Paste several match boxes together to make a chest of drawers. You can assemble boxes in different configurations: Makes a great organizer for small items.

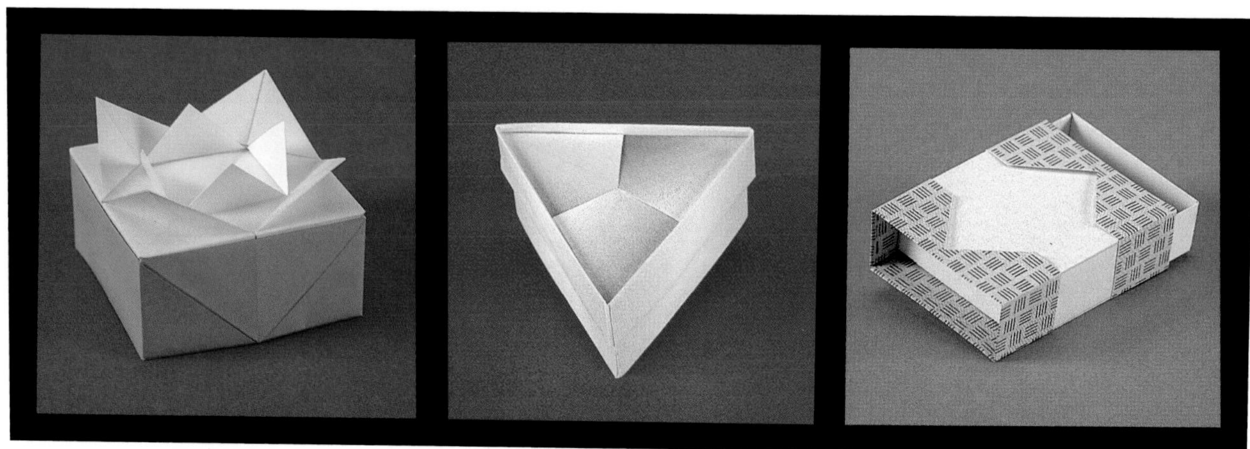

About the Author

Michael G. LaFosse, origami artist and papermaker, has been practicing the art of paper folding for more than 25 years. He teaches, designs, and works as a consultant to museums and schools. His work has been exhibited in galleries and museums across the country.

LaFosse's interest in paper folding began at the age of 7. At the age of 12, he was inspired to begin creating his own original designs, after seeing the extraordinary origami art of Japanese master Akira Yoshizawa. He has since had the opportunity to visit Japan and study with Yoshizawa.

Michael's original origami designs have been featured in books, film, computer programs and designer displays at Symphony Hall in Boston and SAKS Fifth Avenue in New York. Through workshops, videos, and new venues that show his work, LaFosse is bringing the ancient art of origami to a widening audience.

Acknowledgements

I am grateful to Rockport Publishers for allowing me to participate in their paper craft series, and for their encouragement and enthusiasm throughout the project. I especially wish to thank the following people for lending their talent and courteous help in the production of this book: Casandra McIntyre and the people at Rugg Road Papers, Boston, Massachusetts, for bringing my work to the publisher's attention, and for their continued support to the paper arts community at large; Shawna Mullen, for reviewing, editing, and refining the manuscript; Winnie Danenbarger and Barbara States, for shaping the series concept and making timely suggestions along the way; Rosalie Grattaroti, for her enthusiasm in taking care of the many details that connect author and publisher; Douglas Cannon, for his photographic work and advice during the concept stages of production; Michael Lafferty, for his patient work on the "how to" and showcase photography; Ashley Wyatt, for set direction during the step-by-step photography; and Lynne Havighurst, for her artistic direction and for bringing the many elements together beautifully.

Triangle Box Paper Elements 1 of 2

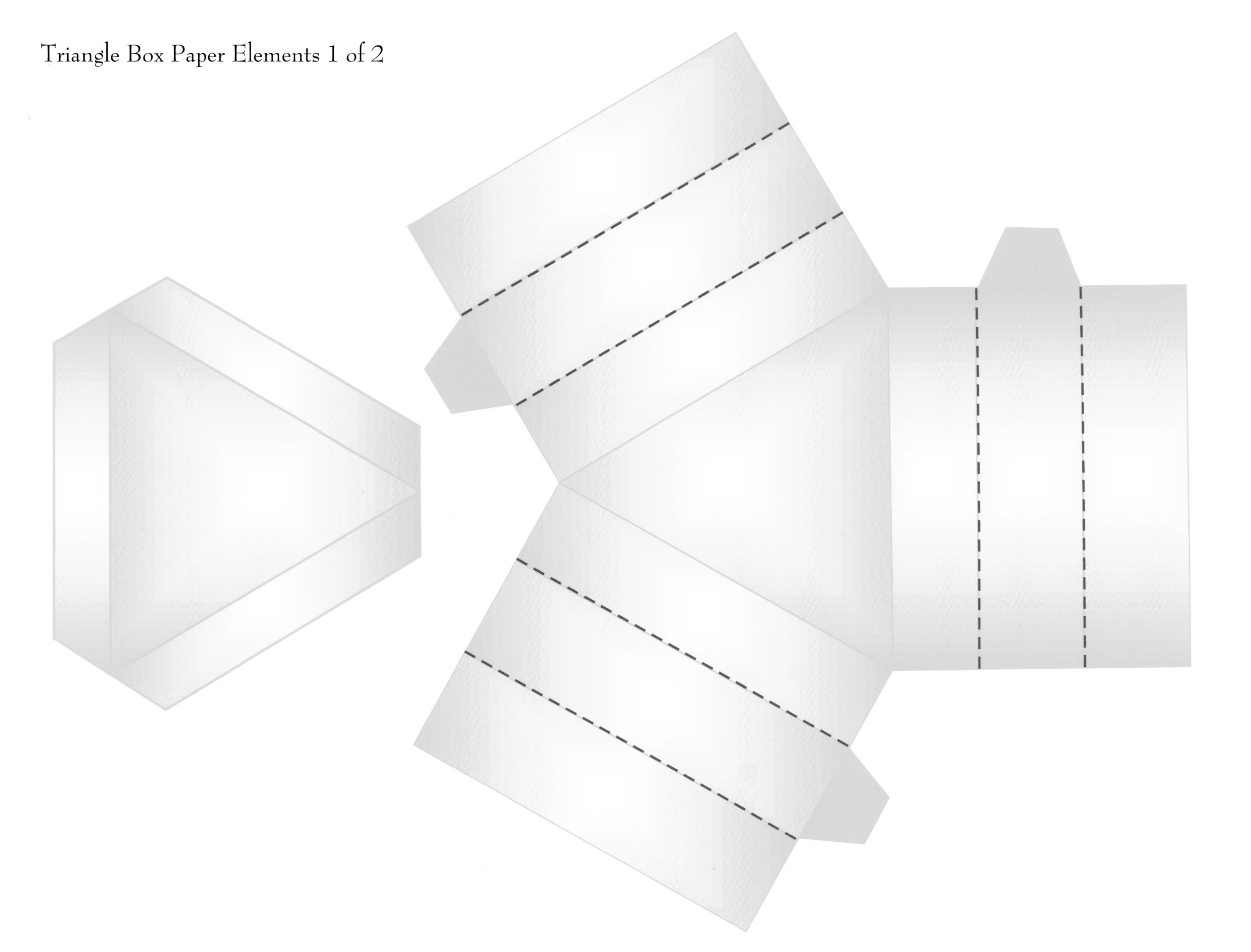

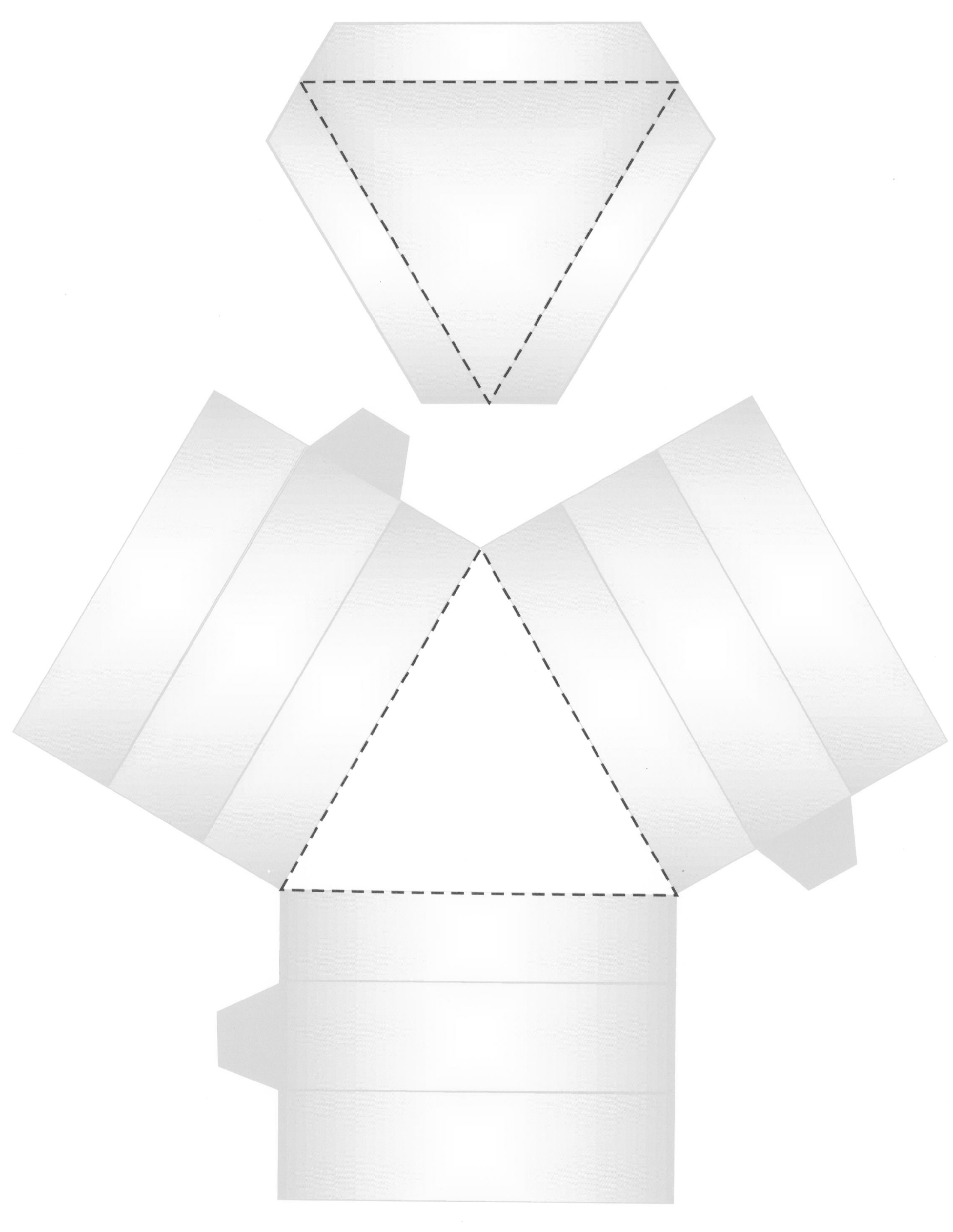

Triangle Box Paper Elements 2 of 2

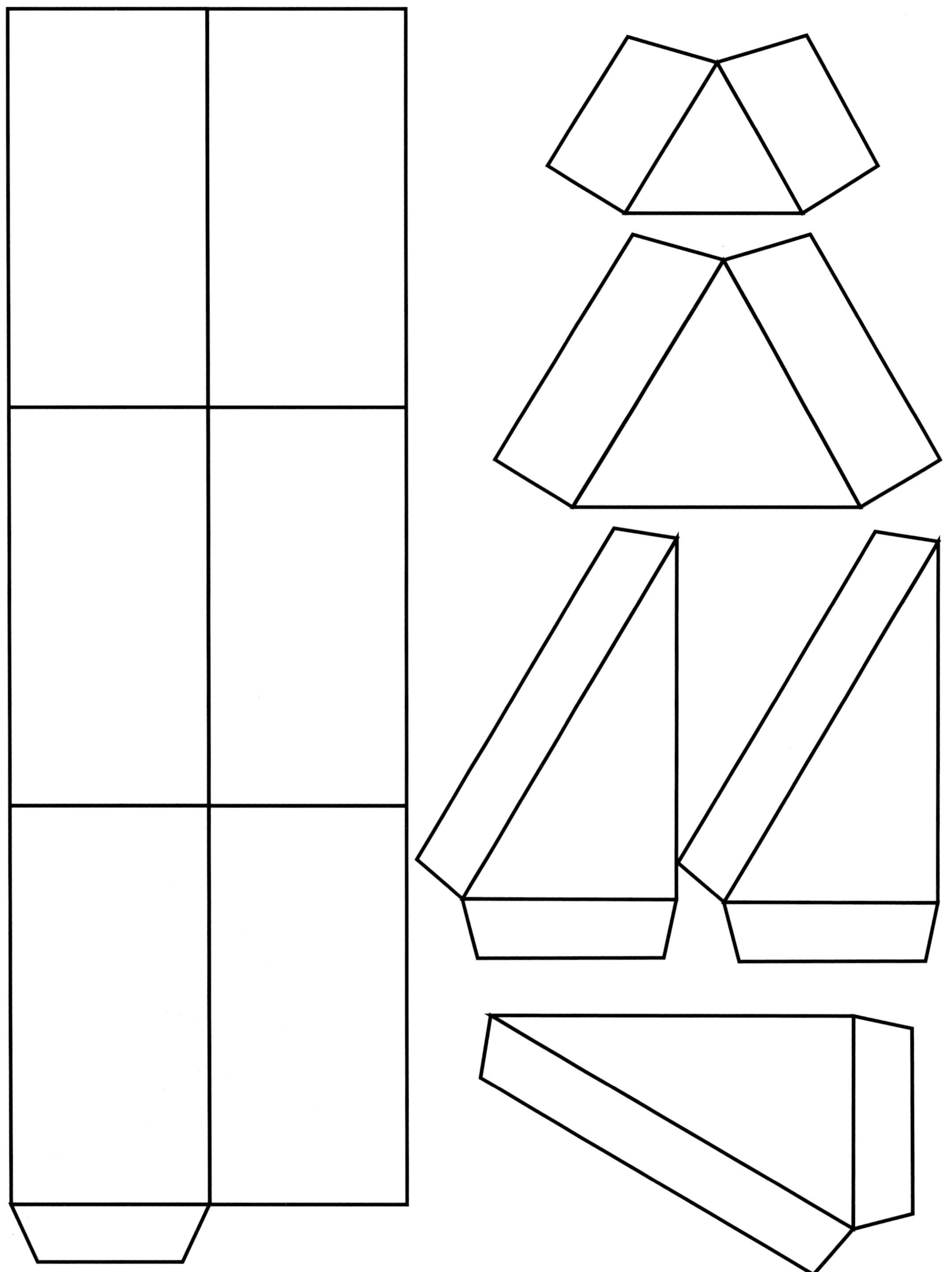

Cube Box Paper Elements 1 of 3

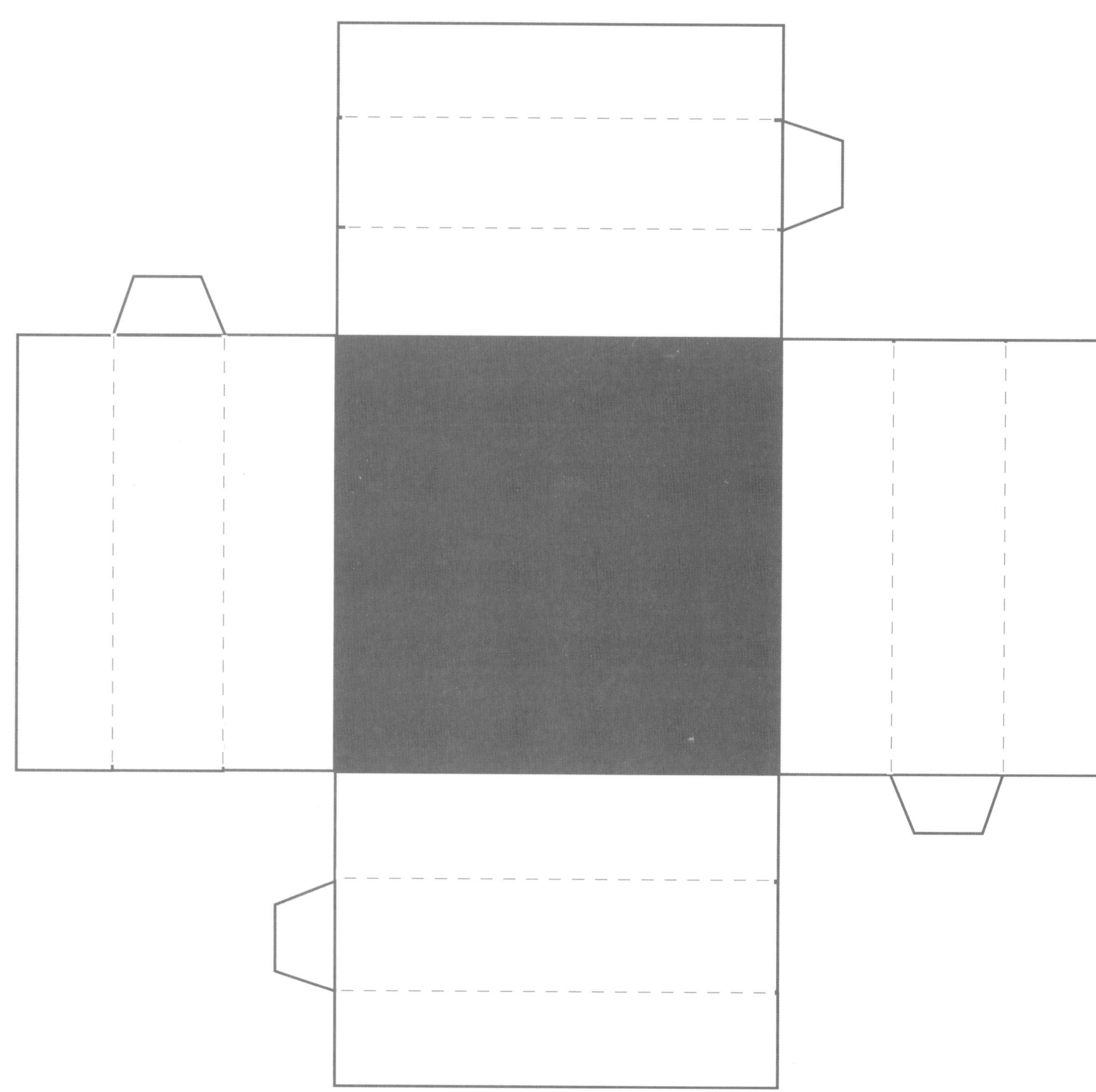

Cube Box Paper Elements 2 of 3

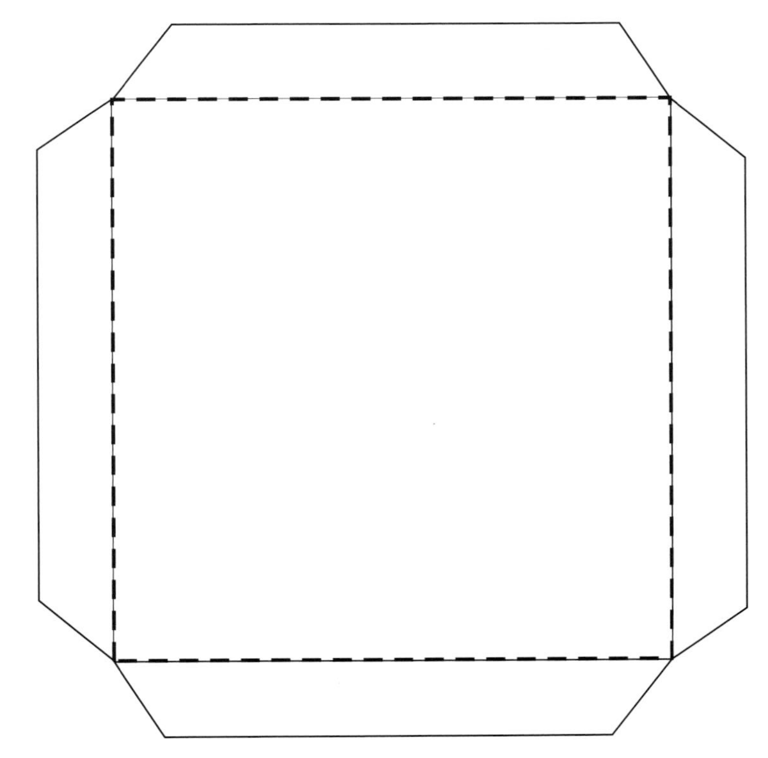

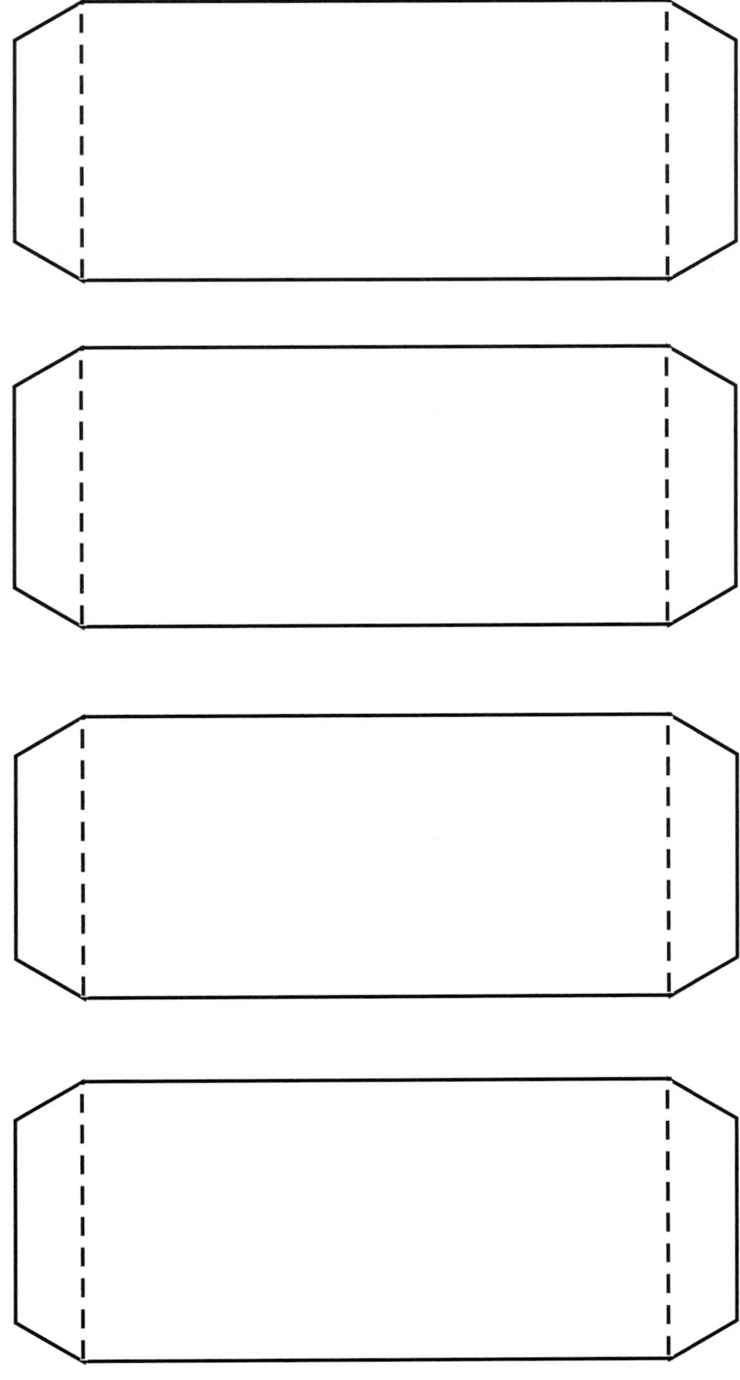

Cube Box Paper Elements 3 of 3

Frame Box Paper Elements 1 of 3

Frame Box Paper Elements 2 of 3

Frame Box Paper Elements 3 of 3

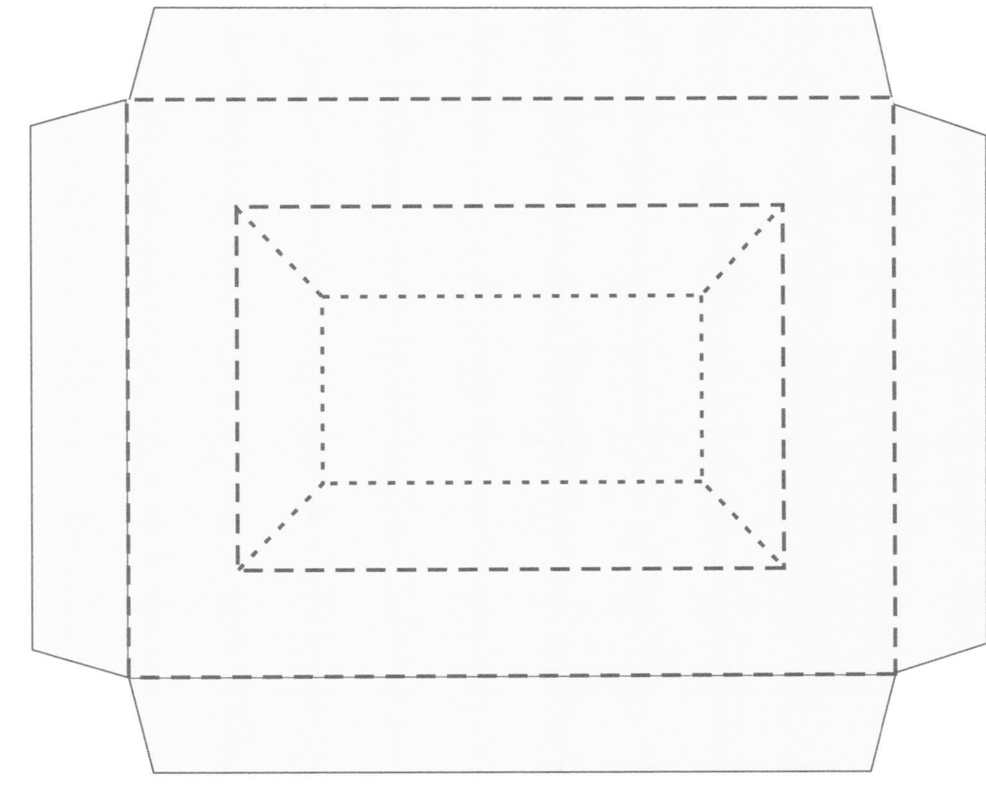

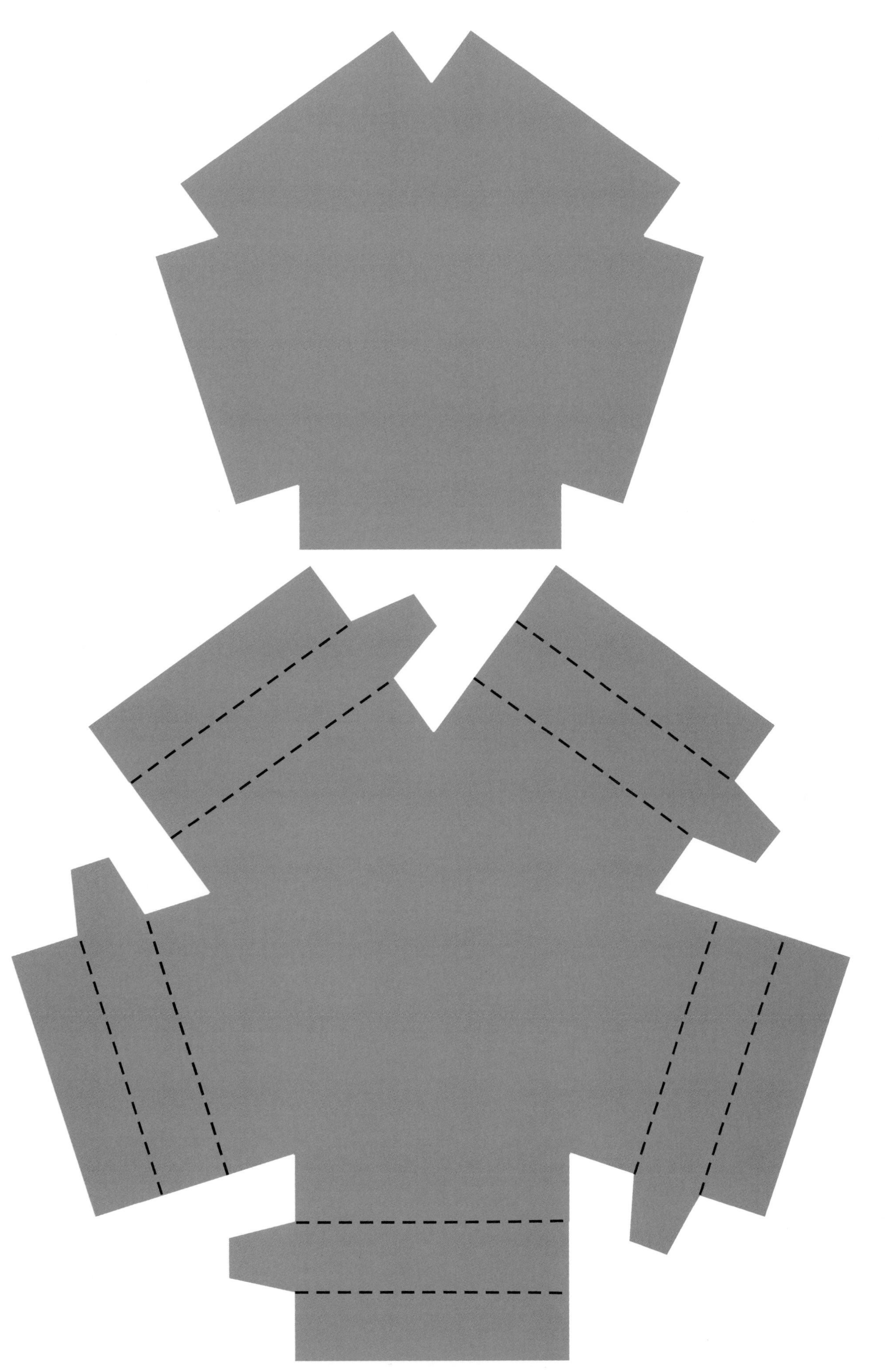

Magician's Box Paper Elements 2 of 2

Puzzle Box Paper Elements 1 of 2

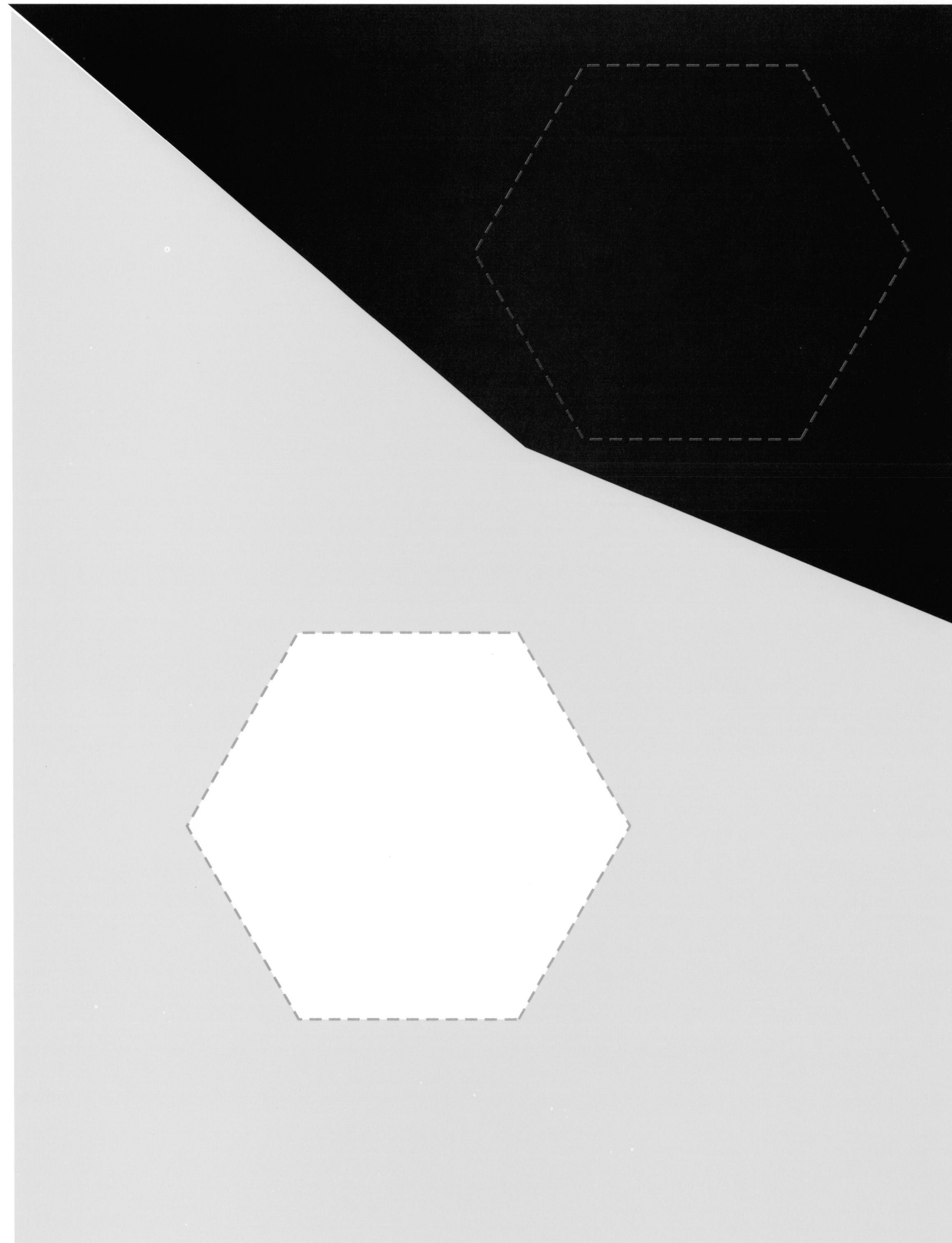

Puzzle Box Paper Elements 2 of 2

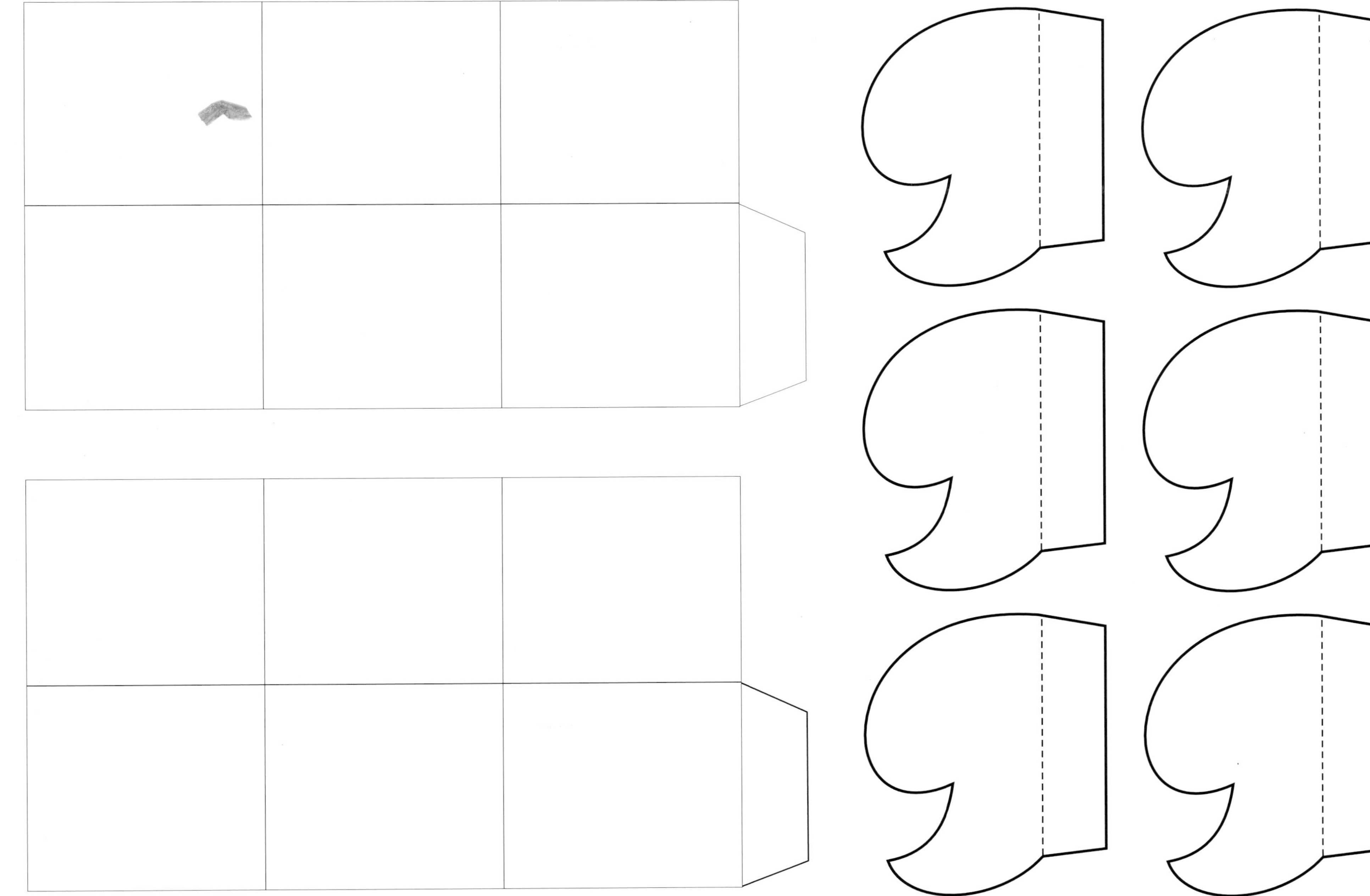

Heart Box Paper Elements 1 of 2

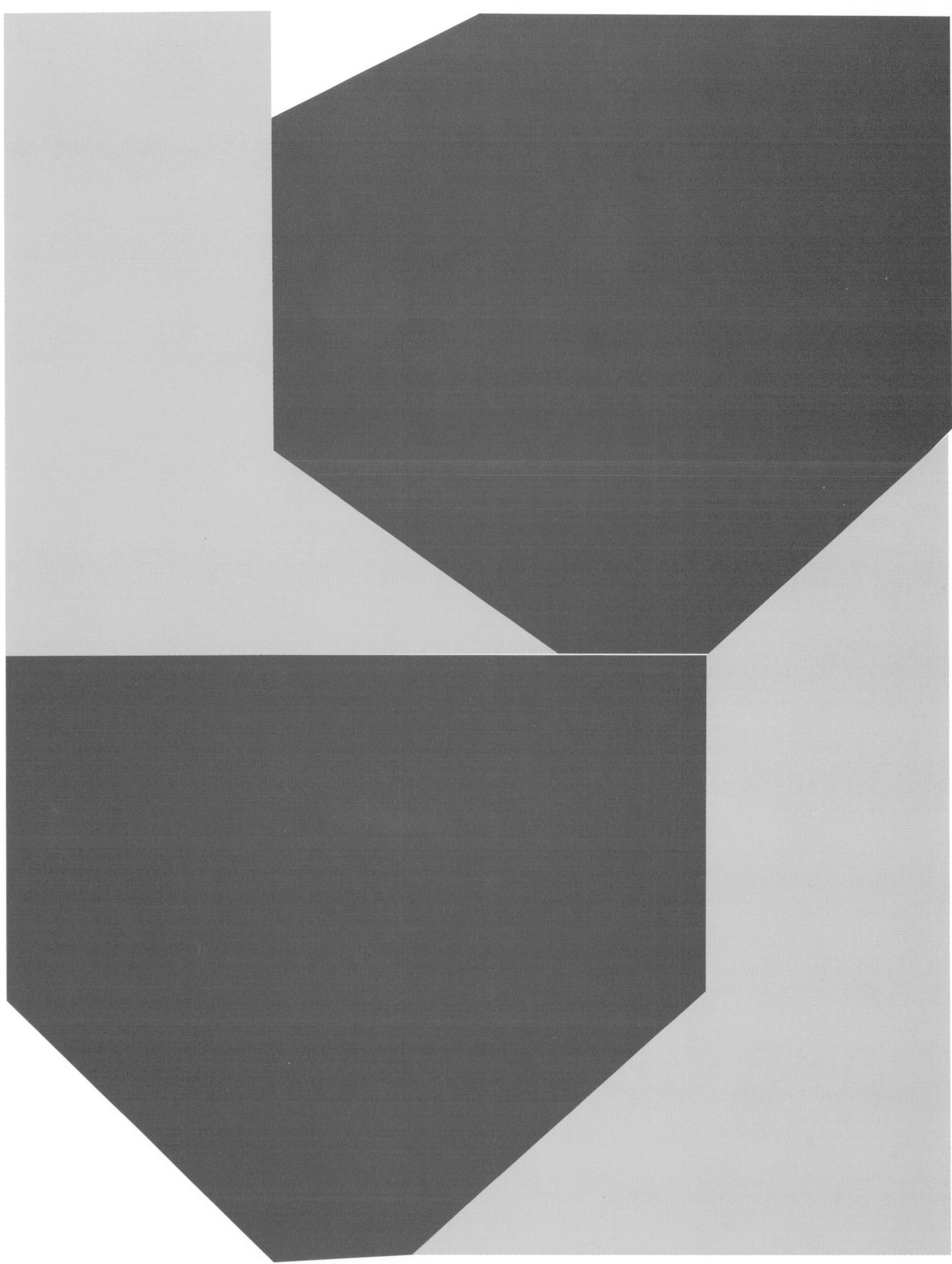

Heart Box Paper Elements 2 of 2

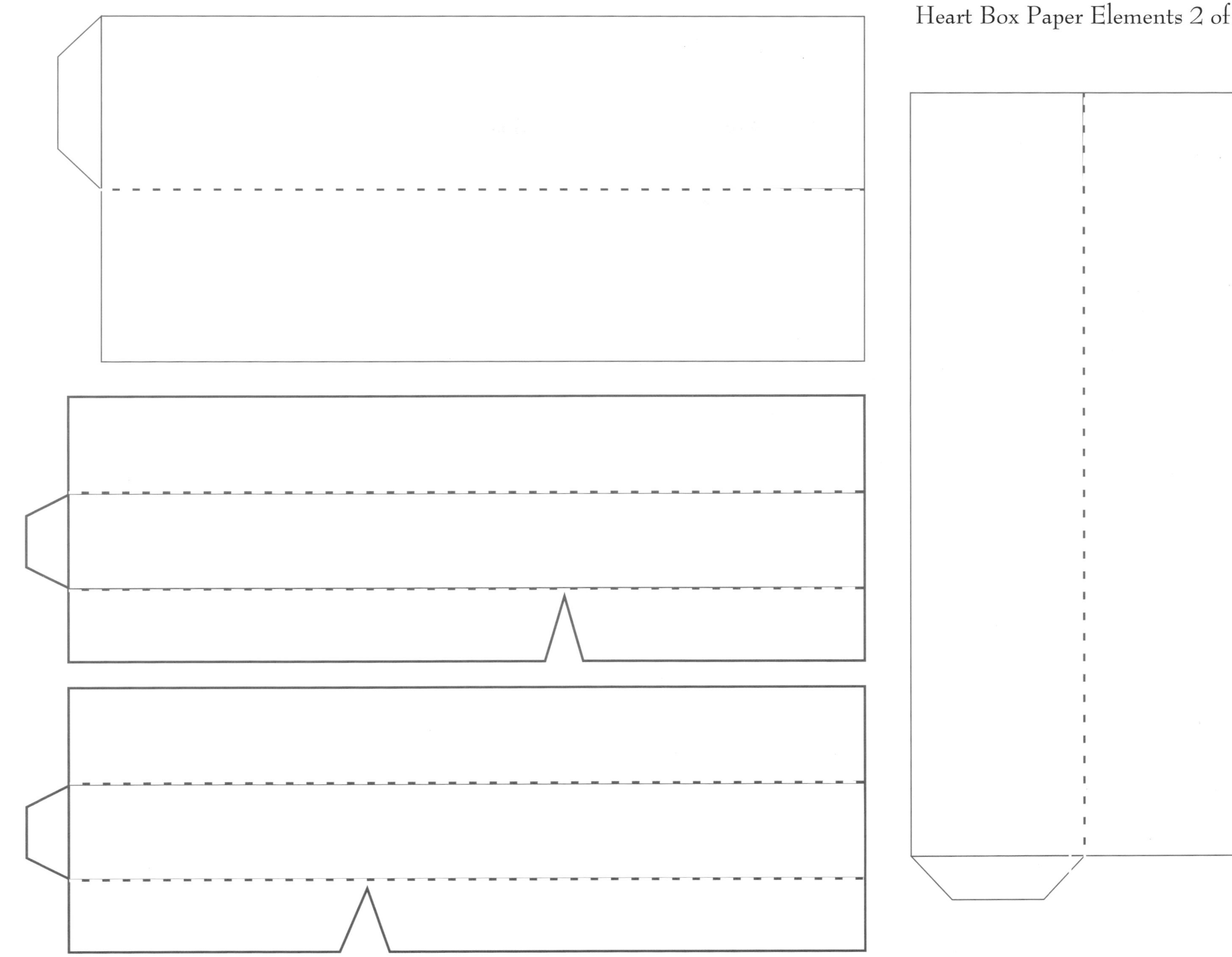

Lotus Box Paper Elements 1 of 3

Lotus Box Paper
Elements 2 of 3

Lotus Box Paper
Elements 3 of 3

Match Box Paper Elements 1 of 2

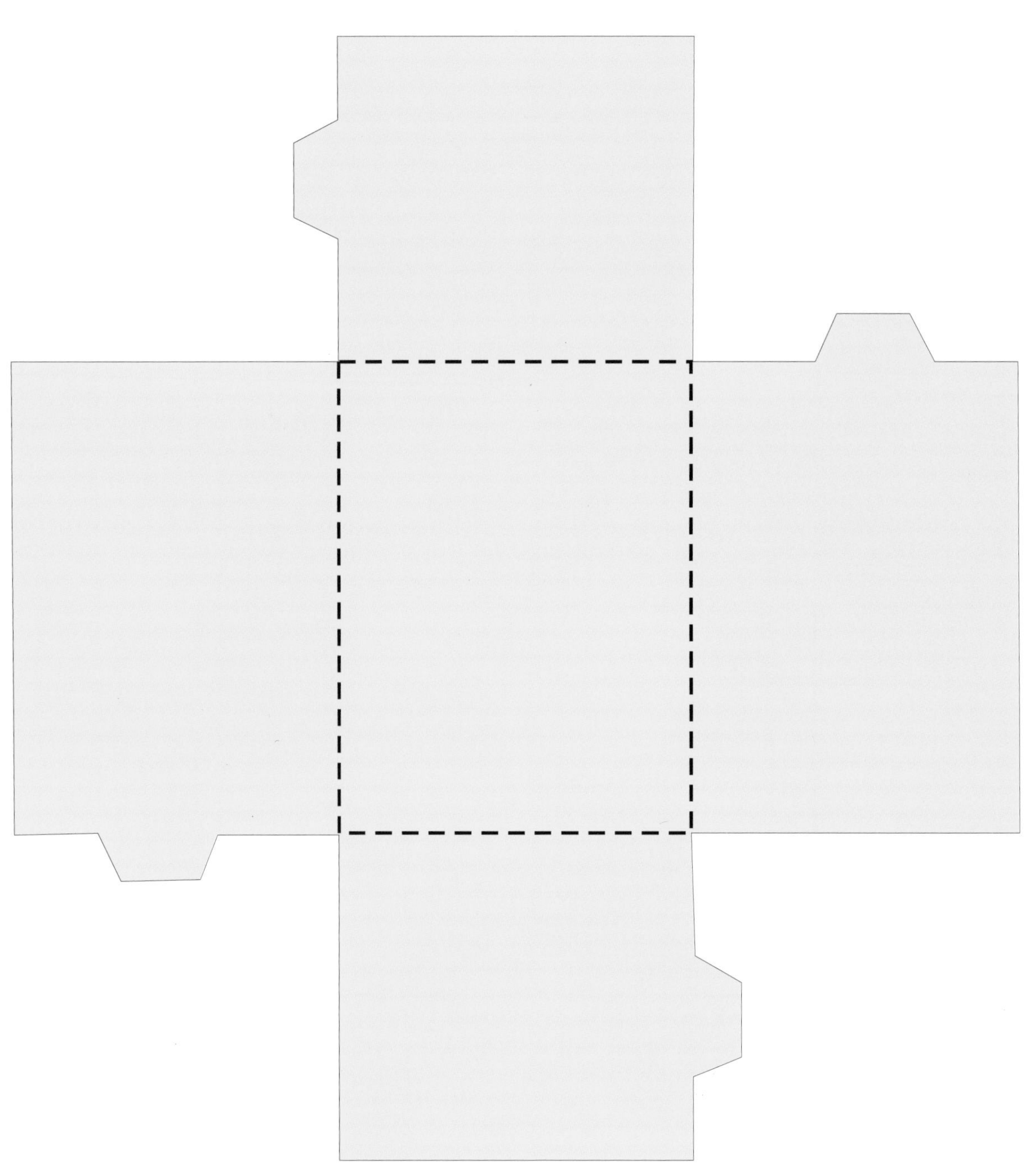

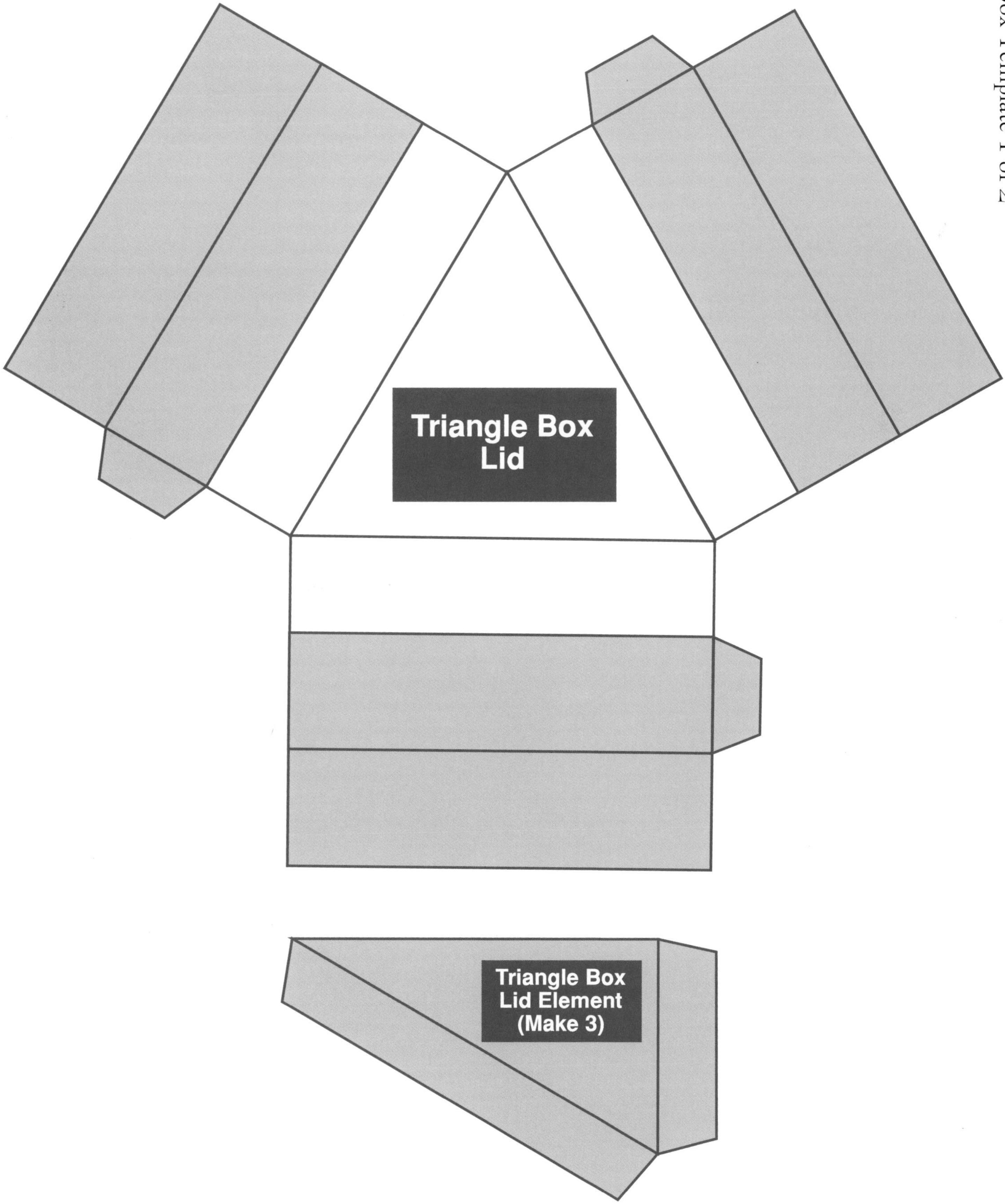

Triangle Box Lid

Triangle Box Lid Element (Make 3)

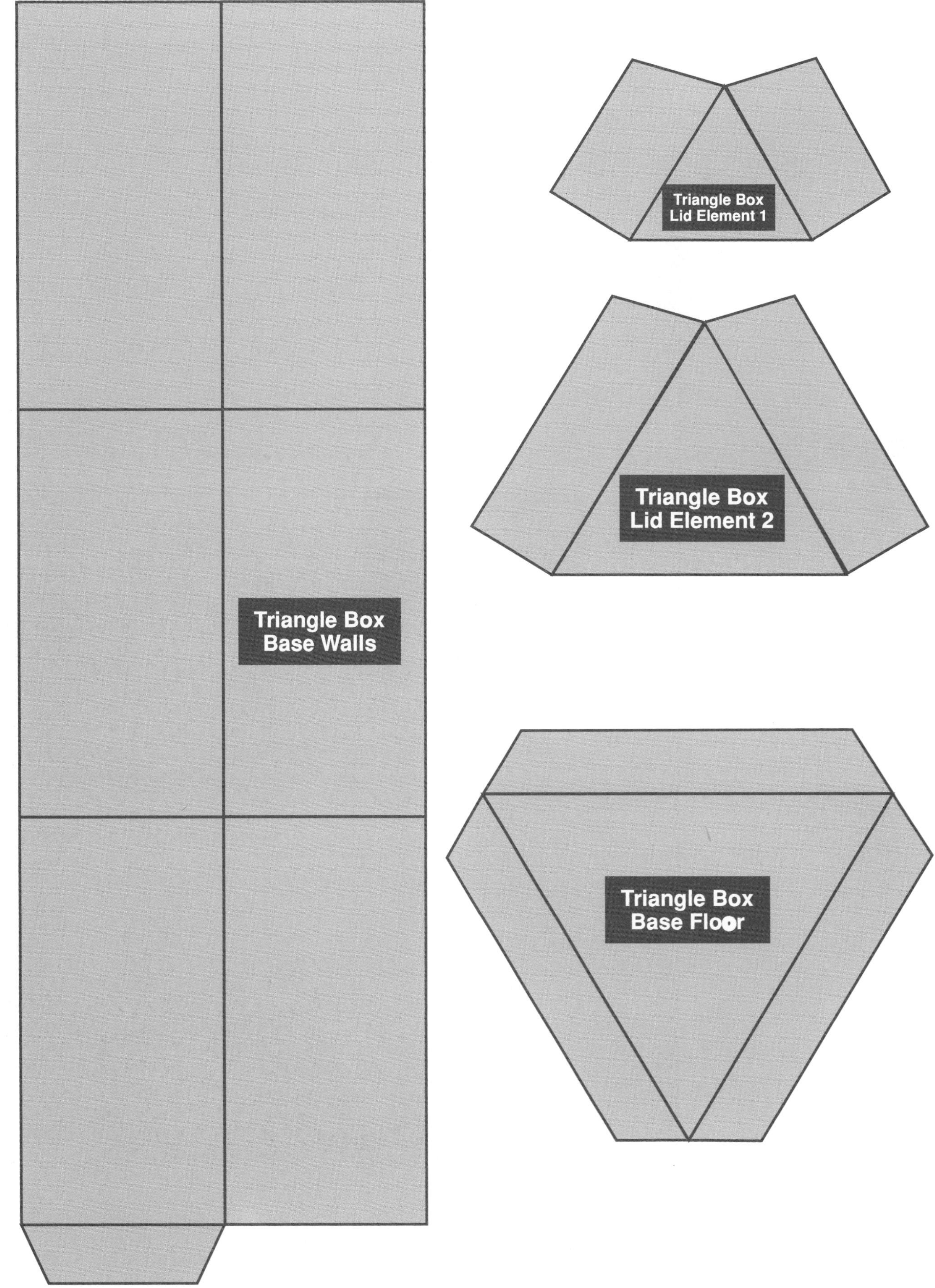
Triangle Box
Lid Element 1
Triangle Box
Lid Element 2
Triangle Box
Base Walls
Triangle Box
Base Floor

Cube Box
Lid

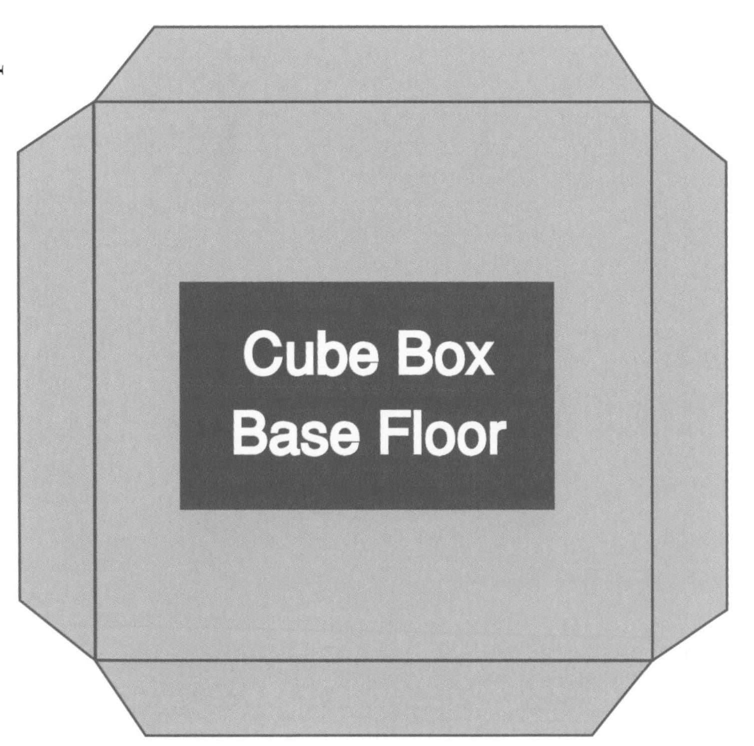
Cube Box
Base Floor

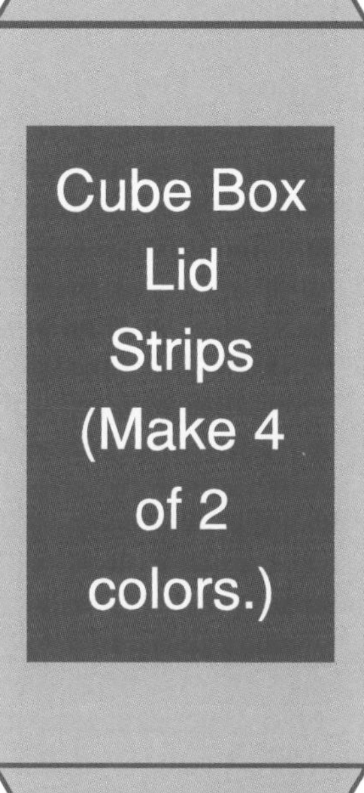
Cube Box
Lid
Strips
(Make 4
of 2
colors.)

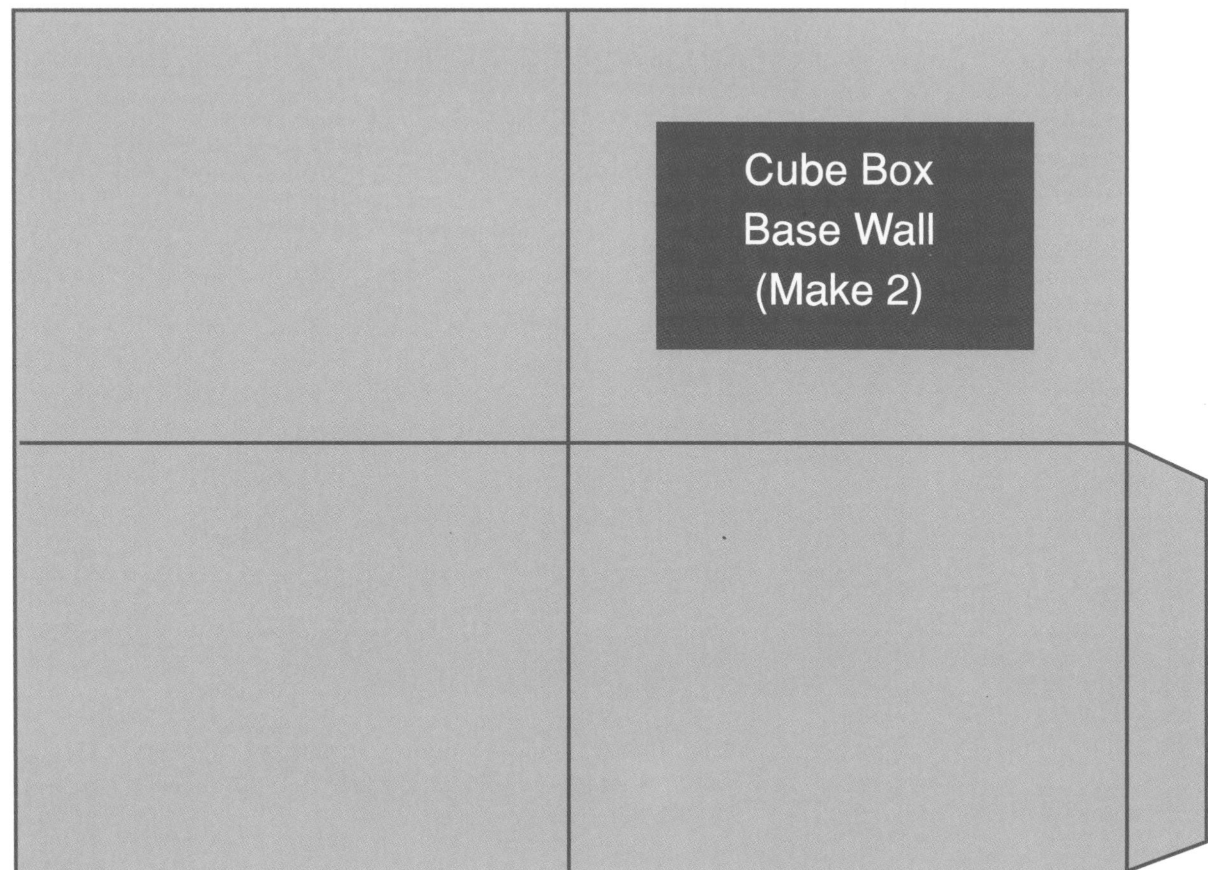
Cube Box
Base Wall
(Make 2)

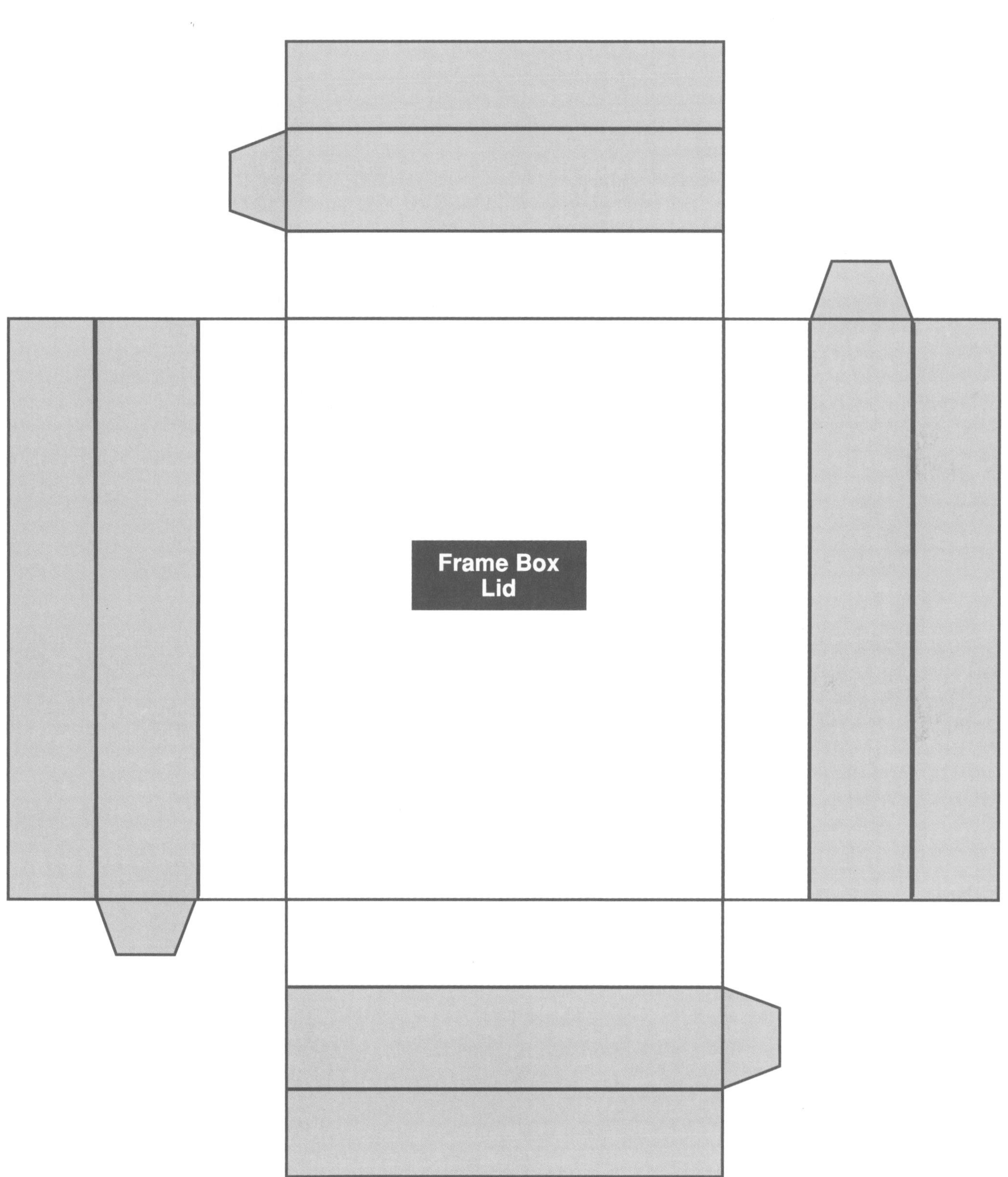
Frame Box
Lid

Frame Box
Base Floor

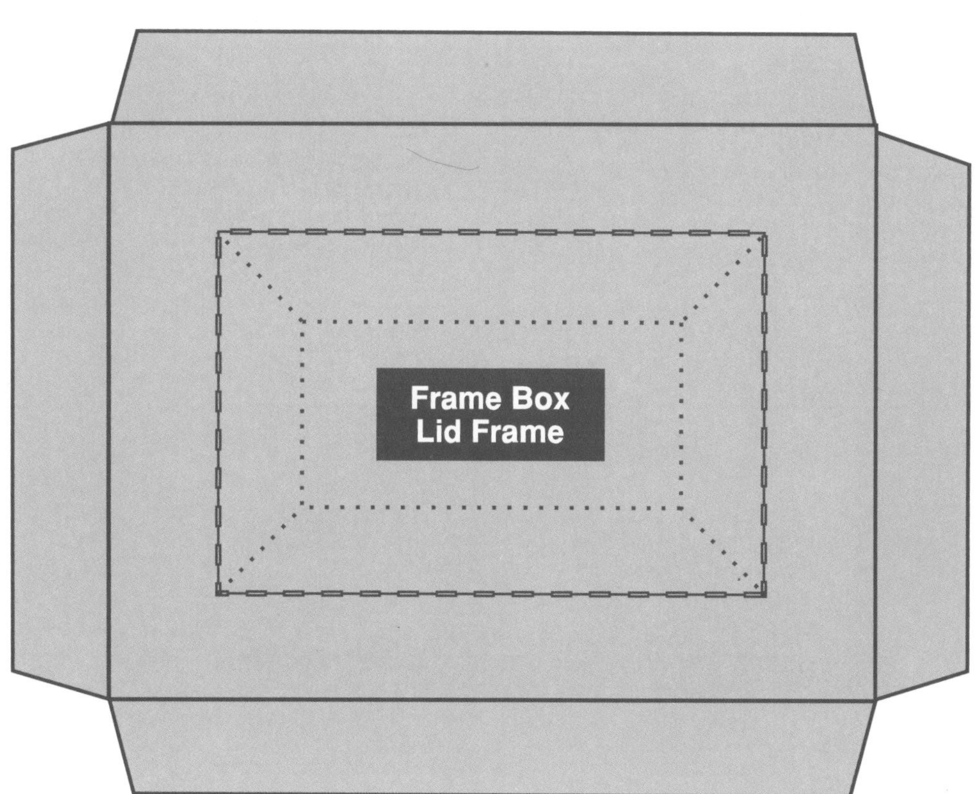
Frame Box
Lid Frame

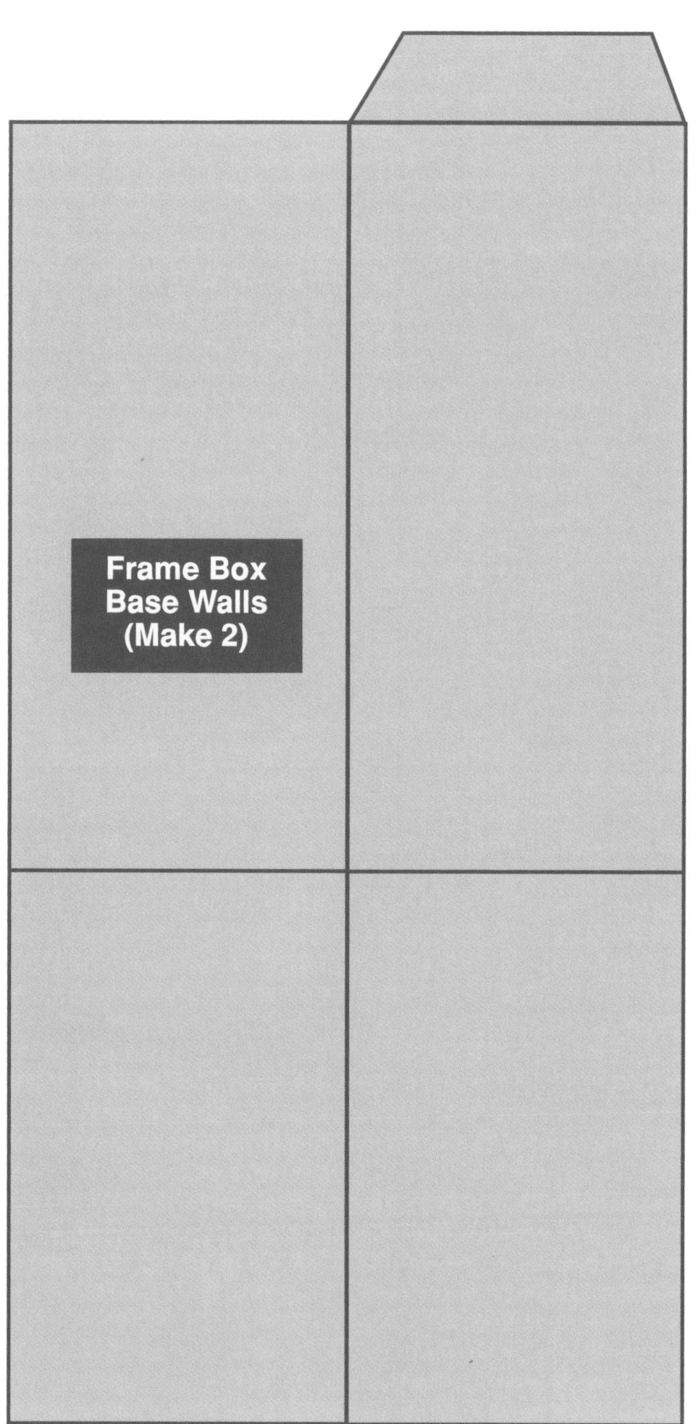
Frame Box
Base Walls
(Make 2)

Magician's Box
Base Wall A

Magician's Box
Base Wall B

Magician's Box
Base Floor

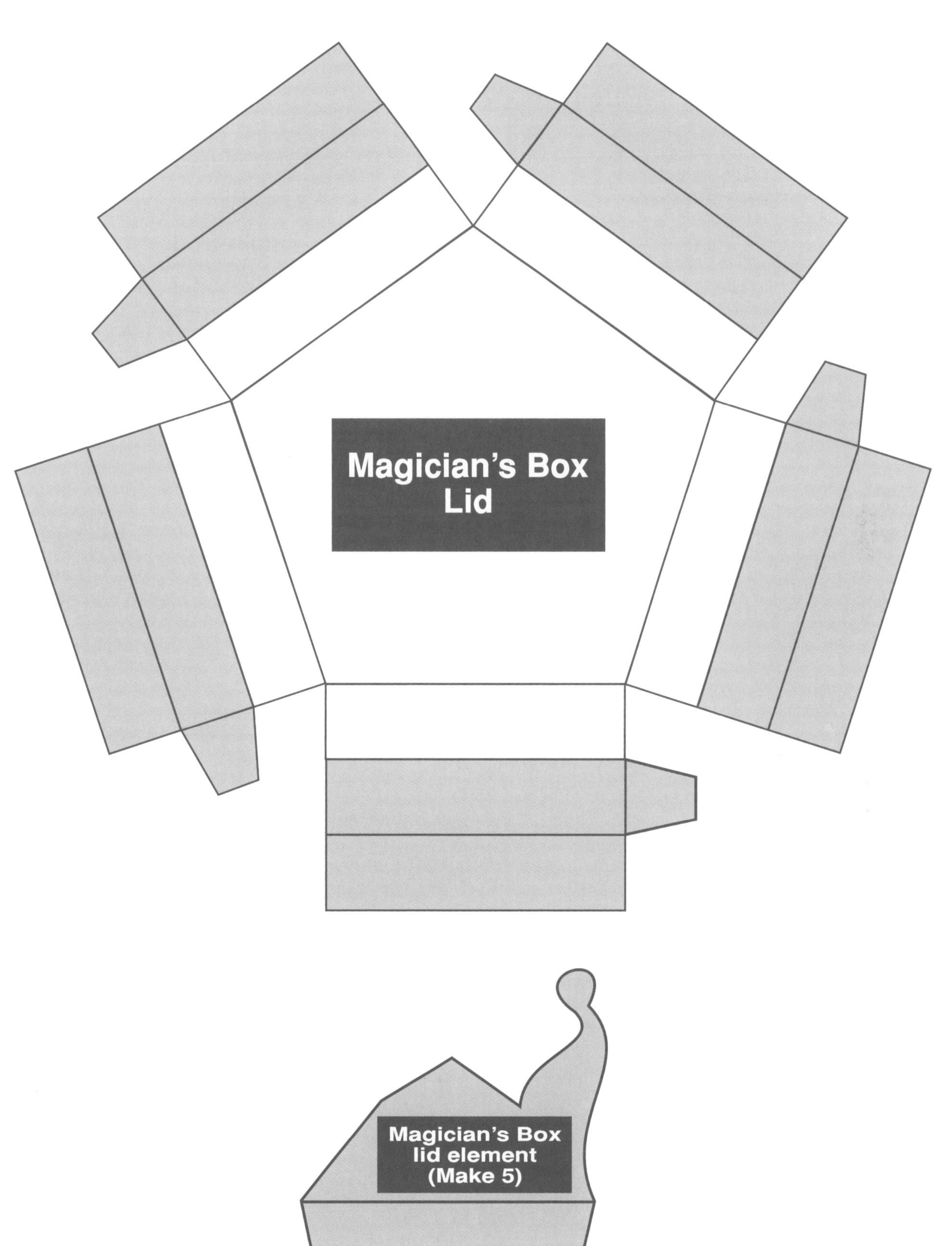
Magician's Box
Lid
Magician's Box
lid element
(Make 5)

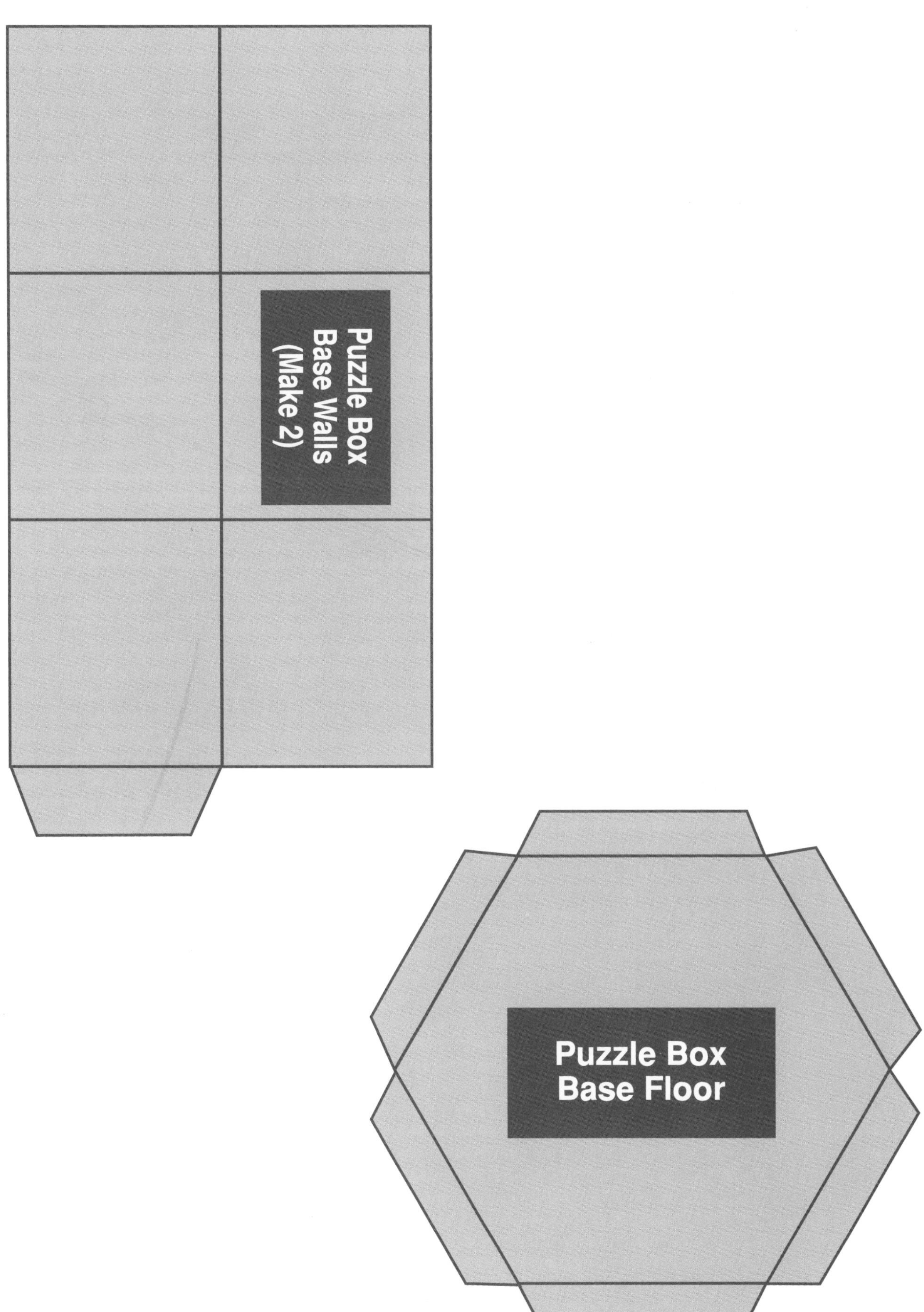
Puzzle Box
Base Walls
(Make 2)
Puzzle Box
Base Floor

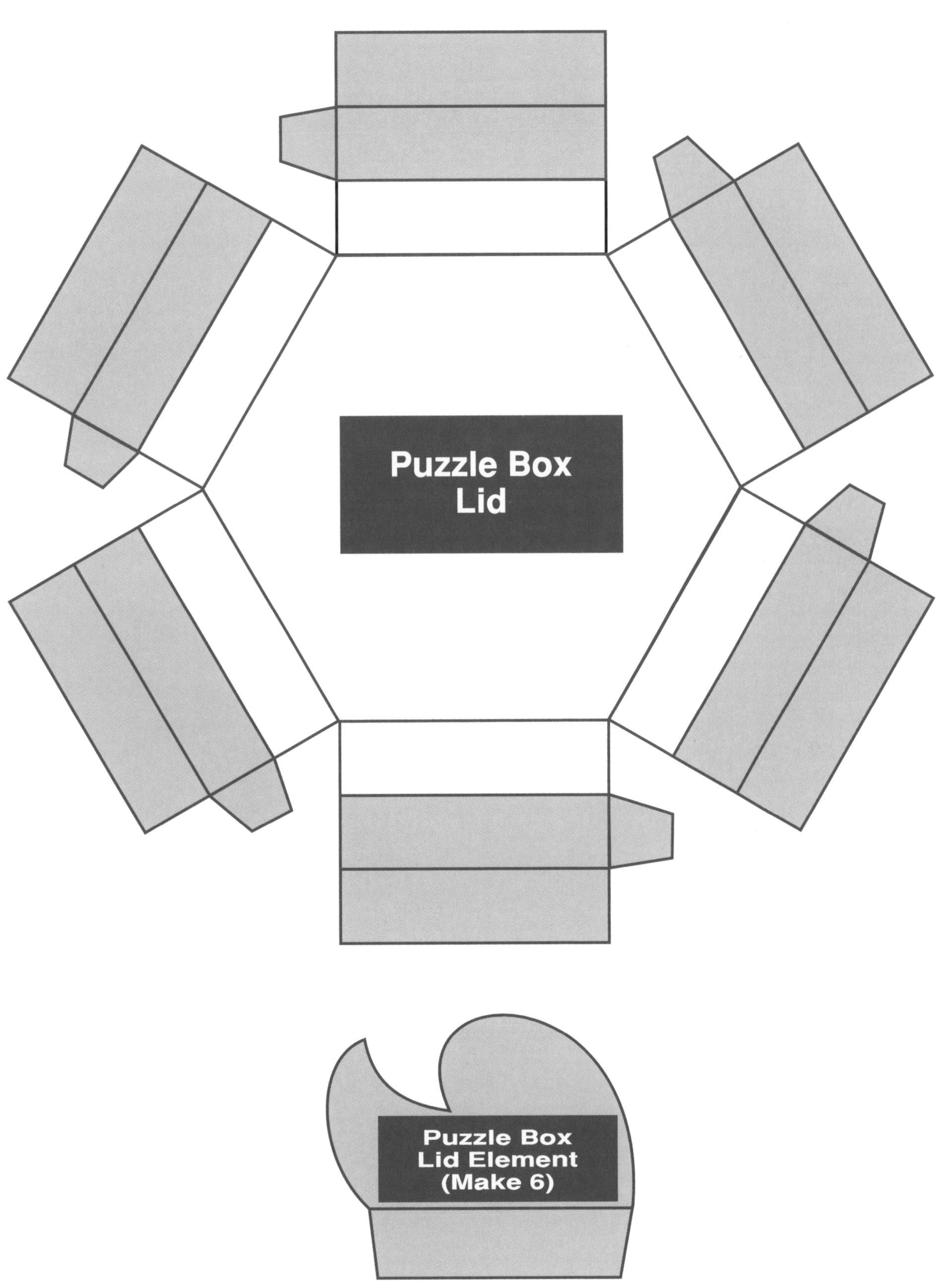
Puzzle Box Lid
Puzzle Box Lid Element (Make 6)

Heart Box
Lid Wall

Heart Box
Lid Wall

Heart Box
Flower
Outer

Heart Box
Flower
Center

Heart Box
Leaf
(Make 3)

Heart Box
Base Wall
(Make 2)

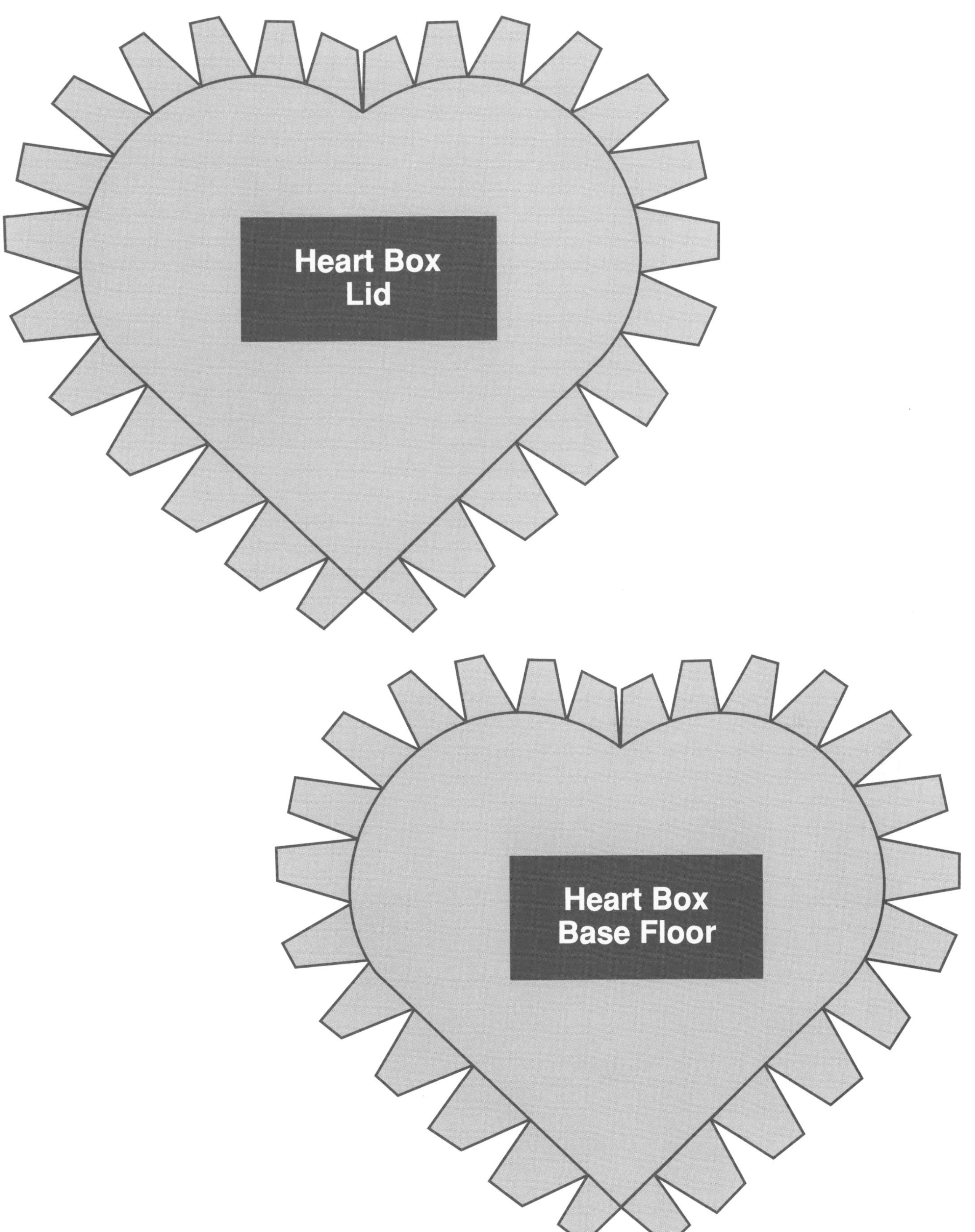
Heart Box
Lid
Heart Box
Base Floor

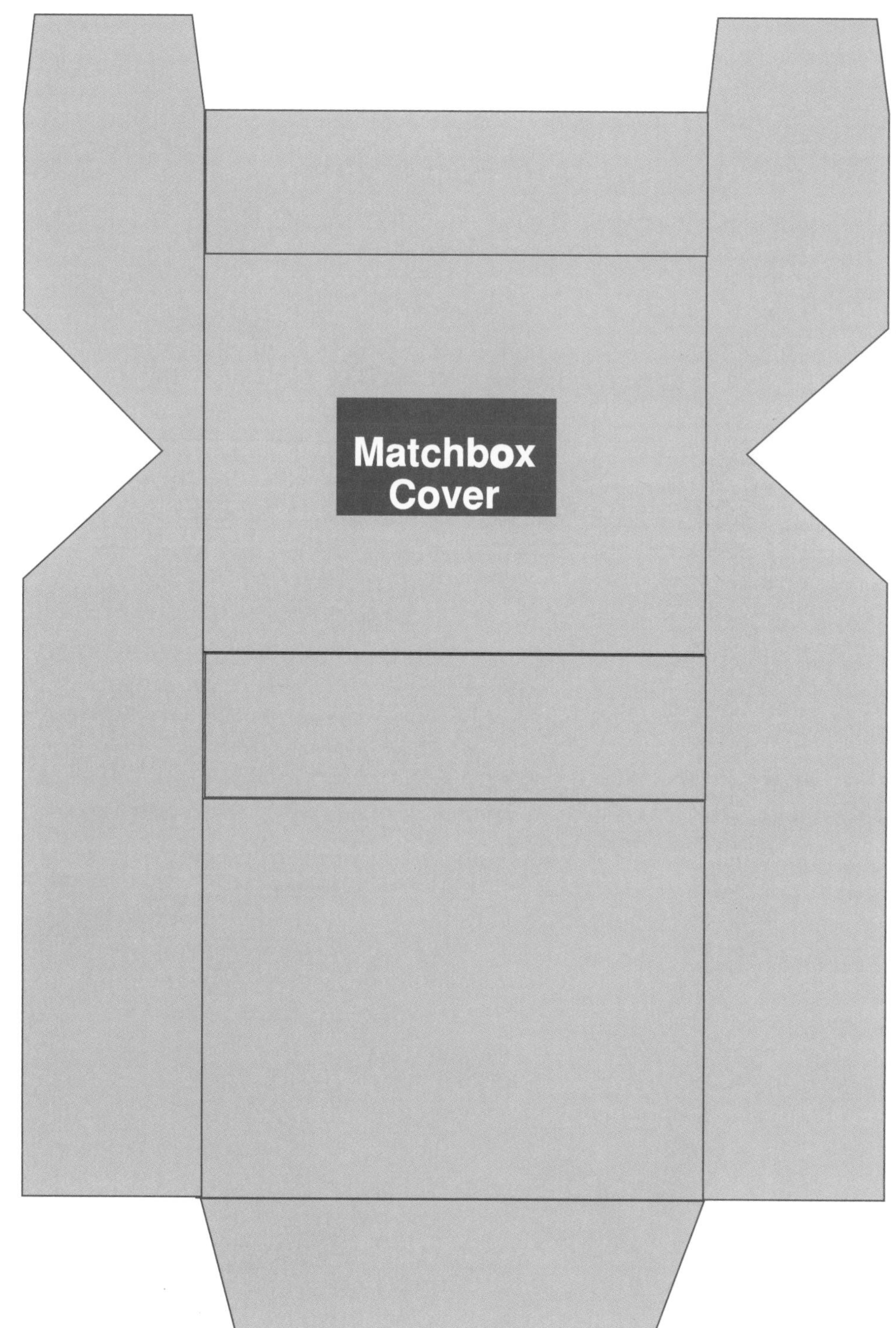
Matchbox
Cover

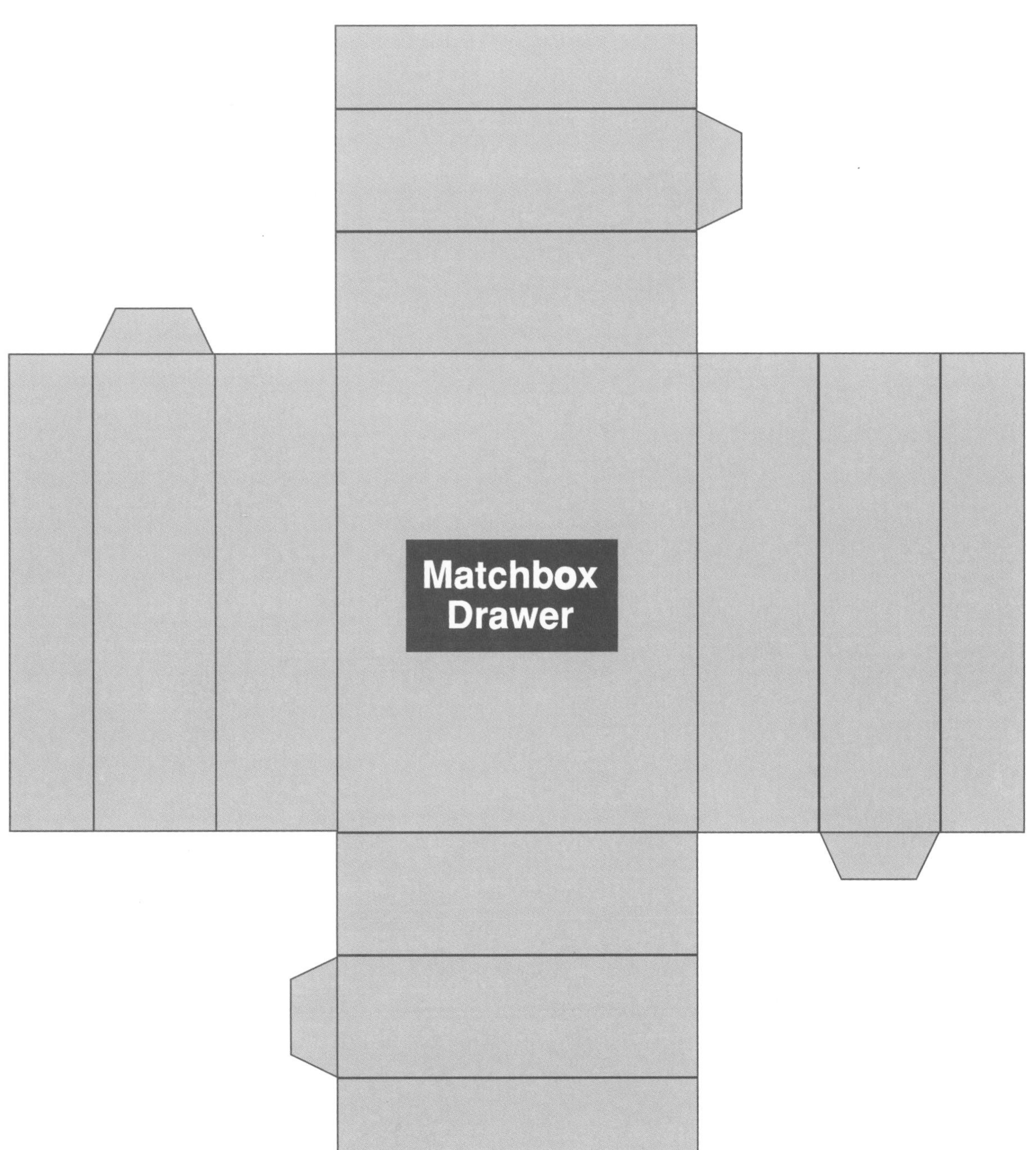
Matchbox
Drawer